FRIENDS WITH THE ENEMY

FRIENDS
WITH
THE
ENEMY

a memoir

VAL MULKERNS

451
Editions

Friends With The Enemy
First Edition, 2017
Published by
451 Editions, Dublin

Trade and order inquiries to:
books@451.ie
www.451Editions.com

© Val Mulkerns 2017

ISBN: 978-1-9999075-3-2

Cover by artist Gerard Calvet: www.gerardcalvet.fr

About the Author

Val Mulkerns is an Irish writer and member of Aosdána. Her first novel, *A Time Outworn*, was released to critical acclaim in Ireland in 1951. She was associate editor and theatre critic for *The Bell* later worked as a journalist and columnist and is often heard on the radio. She is the author of four novels, three collections of short stories, two children's books and many published essays and critical writings. A third edition of her 1984 novel, *The Summerhouse* was published in 2013 and a volume of her selected short stories, *Memory and Desire* was published in 2016. Her memoir, *Friends With The Enemy*, is her eleventh book. She lives in Dublin, Ireland.

For more information please see:

www.valmulkerns.com

1

Summer Entertainment

The place of entertainment that I liked best at one stage of my childhood was the old churchyard in Drumcondra. It was a cheerful leafy place where the birds never stopped singing and where there was a deep well, surrounded by rose bushes, which you approached by descending three or four mossy steps. An old zinc watering can was always left at the bottom of the steps for the use of mourners and, when you had finished tidying the family grave, that watering can was always left back. Like the steps, it too was partly clothed in moss and likewise the old jugs that stood around it.

James Gandon, English-born architect of the Custom House and other city masterpieces, is buried there but this was not the reason for our frequent visits. If you stood with your back to the door of the neat small church belonging to the Church of Ireland, the exceedingly tidy graves with imposing headstones to your right belonged to Protestants, and those on your left to certain Roman Catholics. My maternal grandparents, by ancient residential rights, were among those permitted to be buried on the left-hand side. They lay beneath a yew tree and a small marble headstone which had to be scraped white again after the winter rains. Their engraved names were cleaned with a toothpick or a nailfile: Frank was quite easy, but Margaret could be tricky.

This, however, was not my job. My job was to fetch water from the old well, a place I really loved. Shady, green and mysterious, its mossy steps could be cold on sandalled feet in summer, but on hot days I liked to kneel down and splash my face with water which I always believed must be green. It disappointed me to find that every drop had dried out clear and clean when I inspected my face in the mirror at home later. You sometimes heard and even saw a robin among the straggle of rose bushes that surrounded the well and it was tempting to linger in that cool place, among the rusty jugs and the watering can and the large wire litter baskets into which you threw the previous week's flowers – that was part of my job too.

Often on a hot day, I would eke out the job and by the time I got back, with my cotton dress soaking wet, my mother would be deep in conversation with an old man who kept the most extraordinary grave in Drumcondra. It was about four graves wide and there was no headstone. Instead, there were four white-painted wooden posts with white chains hanging between them, and a few wooden crosses bearing family names which the old man often repainted in black. Between these crosses and separating them was a maze of tiny box hedges. I clearly remembered the grave when years later I saw an Elizabethan knot garden in Hampton Court.

Of course the old man in Drumcondra had made a much more ornate horizontal garden of his family plot. Inside the tiny box squares were all sorts of things – little bridges of seashells, a pair of white clasped hands, infant angels kneeling with bowed heads, small sprays of immortelles, and many horizontal crosses, as well as the vertical ones. He had taken care to plant only small seasonal flowers inside his box hedges, so that nothing was ever out of proportion. There were forget-me-nots, crocuses, pansies, dwarf irises, grape hyacinths and primroses right through the summer.

The labour was obviously considerable. Whenever we went, he was always there, weeding, deadheading, watering or planting. Presumably his family, all dead, had been a source of company to him in life and in death had become the same. He and my mother got on very well, exchanging pleasantries about the weather as they worked but also, now and again, fragments of their respective family histories. He told her about his red-haired sister Alice who had caught a cold at Parnell's funeral in 1891 and died soon afterwards of pneumonia, and she told him about *her* sister, who was frequently missing during school holidays when the family sat down to midday dinner. 'Go and look across the road in the churchyard,' my grandfather would say grimly, and right here sure enough Nora would be found, with a black ribbon around her straw hat, crying her eyes out at some stranger's funeral and being comforted by unknown people who gave her chocolate and took her to be a distant cousin – one of themselves, anyhow.

I remember the old man's hearty laugh ringing out over the murmuring of the students at their Divine Office behind the wall of All Hallows College, and I also remember the day the old man wasn't there any more. Three weeks in a row he wasn't there, and then one day we found his masterpiece of a memorial garden tumbled and ruined, a new grave having been dug among the miniatures, and the earth tossed back roughly. There obviously wasn't anyone to beautify *his* grave and so gradually the box hedges grew over it, making a pretty enough mound of miniature green leaves.

Frank and Margaret O'Neill, my maternal grandparents, were more fortunate in the matter of grave maintenance. They had, apart from my mother, five other living children who were the product of a rather odd mixed marriage – and a very romantic one in fact. She was a Protestant, a Miss Healy, who belonged to a business family in Dame Street. Margaret had cousins in New York whom she kept begging her parents to visit. When she finished boarding school at seventeen, they arranged a travelling companion for her, a trustworthy young fellow of twenty, who happened to be Roman Catholic but who had already been across the Atlantic. His father was among the dispatch staff in Dame Street and it so happened that young Frank was planning to emigrate to better himself, as the saying went. Frank and Margaret got on very well in the course of the voyage to New York and he regaled her with funny stories of his life as a copy boy for *The Freeman's Journal*. He had hopes of doing better in the New World, he told her. By the time the ship berthed in New York harbour, they had fallen in love and Margaret didn't see home again for five years. By that time she and Frank were married and he was working as a junior reporter for the *New York Herald Tribune*. I could never work out why they came back home to Dublin, but they arrived in time for the birth of their first child, and shortly afterwards Frank O'Neill got a job on *The Freeman's Journal* as a staff reporter.

All I remember about Margaret is her voice, and the place where she used to hide a paper bag of bulls' eyes or dolly mixture for me (under the cushion of her rocking chair) in the front parlour of their home in Drumcondra. She died when I was three in 1928, but my grandfather Frank lived on for five more years. He was a short, rather breathless little man with a brick red face, a fiery moustache and very bright, very challenging blue eyes under his bowler hat. He was mad about cars and owned a Model T Ford in which he often took us to Sutton for summer picnics or to Glendalough when the leaves began to drift down on the lakes. He had the sort of death I think he would have chosen for himself. He was trying to crank up an even older car one day in his coach house out at the back, and (in the opinion of my father) she had probably kicked harder than he had expected. He was thrown backwards and died of a heart attack. But the point is, my father always said, that all he would have been aware of is that he *did* succeed in starting up the old engine again. So he must have died in triumph, aged almost eighty.

There was a sound friendship between my father, Jimmy Mulkerns, and that old man. It was said (although not by her sisters) that Esther, my mother, was his favourite daughter and it must have been a wry satisfaction to him that she brought in the right sort of son-in-law, a lively cultured young patriot who was a voracious reader. His family was working-class, but he had had the gumption to educate himself after leaving school at the age of fourteen. As a young railwayman, he had saved up to take elocution lessons from the Abbey actor Frank Fay and had succeeded so well that W.B. Yeats had chosen him to play Michael in one of the early productions of *The Land of Heart's Desire*. He had actually been invited to tea in Drumcondra Road by one of the older O'Neill girls, but had fallen in love with her little sister. By that time Jimmy Mulkerns was heavily involved in the National Movement and was impressed by the 'safe house' status of the Drumcondra house. The boys of that family were not politically minded, but they were accustomed now and again to bring home friends on the run from the Black and Tans for a meal and a night's rest – former schoolfellows, some of them, like Mike Hoolihan.

The story I like best – a story I heard as a child when I sat down on the stairs to listen one night on my way up to bed – is about the same Mike Hoolihan. He came in, exhausted, with my Uncle Frank O'Neill one evening and threw himself down on the hard horsehair sofa in the back parlour after hanging up his coat in the hall. Unable to stay awake long enough for the sandwiches, which my mother had been dispatched to make for him down in the kitchen, he lay as one dead in the back parlour with his shock of black hair flopped over his face and one leg dangling to the floor. The arrival of my mother with a tray of sandwiches coincided with a thunderous series of bangs at the door and shouted threats that it would be broken down if it wasn't opened at once.

By the time four or five Black and Tans had stormed in, young Esther had spread the voluminous makings of new

Easter curtains over the sleeping Mike and was busy with a pair of scissors and a measuring tape preparing to cut the cloth. She disarmed the Black and Tans with a smile and an offer of the sandwiches which she said she had just made for her father who was due home soon from his night shift at the *Freeman's Journal*. The thugs snatched a sandwich each before making a charge upstairs to search the rest of the house. The climax of the story came after the raiders had left. They had not only missed Mike Hoolihan under the curtains but they had also missed Mike Hoolihan's greatcoat hanging up on the hallstand, and they had missed his revolver bulging from one pocket! The loud guffaws of my uncles were such, my mother always said, as almost to bring the raiders back again, but by then they were probably roaring off across Drumcondra Bridge bound for The Cat and Cage, where perhaps some of The Boys could be found over a peaceful pint.

The Boys? It was never necessary to explain what boys. This was the very early nineteen twenties, towards the end of the War of Independence, near enough to the romantic dream of Easter 1916 in which my father had played his part. He was not like some of the Volunteers, too young at the time to know what he was doing. He was already well into his thirties and had a job on the Midland and Great Western Railway. More important to him, he was beginning to be known as a balladeer and had a little volume called *Songs of Freedom* published by the Music Depot in Mary Street. More important still, I think, to him: he was beginning to get walk-on parts in the Abbey Theatre. He had, in fact, something to lose, and he lost it.

But he gained the passionate attachment of Essie O'Neill which did indeed last until death did them part. Hers. In order to make marriage with Esther possible, he gave up his artistic ambitions and took a sensible job as a salesman in the General Electric Company, Trinity Street, with a salary just about big enough to rent them a flat in Grove Park, Rathmines, which provided me with ducks to feed as a small child in the nearby curve of the Grand Canal known as Portobello Harbour.

I was fascinated to learn not long ago that, even as a man of business, Jimmy Mulkerns did not detach himself from the Movement, but was of valuable service to Michael Collins in 13 Trinity Street. My father was a man who knew how to hold his tongue where necessary, despite his passion for storytelling. But as an old man close to death, he told the Collins story to his elder son, my brother Jim, who told it to his daughter Helena. She was working as a freelance journalist in New York and she wrote it up for the 1997 St Patrick's week edition of *The Irish Echo*, which is how it came to me. I did know that both my parents were Pro-Treaty and bitterly resentful of Eamon de Valera for having stood back from his instruction to Collins to 'make the best terms you can, Mick' and to have caused the Civil War after Collins had done just that. Both parents believed that Collins had been disgracefully betrayed and later murdered.

2

Two Schools

The school I think of as my school was the Dominican College, Eccles Street, one of a series of convent boarding schools which had expanded from one or two Georgian houses into maybe five or six others. These schools were The Sacred Heart, Leeson Street, Loreto on St Stephen's Green and my own. They all smelled much the same – as I discovered when we exchanged audiences for plays and concerts. They smelled of lavender-waxed corridors and fresh linen, of snuffed candles and sharpened pencils, of wafting incense, drifting down from the windows of convent chapels. They smelled of libraries and learning. In fact, it was the Junior Library in Eccles Street that finally broke my mother's taboo on borrowing books. How could you possibly associate noxious bugs and hideous infections with a school library that smelled sweetly of the convent?

And so the glories of *Jane Eyre* and *David Copperfield* were revealed to me for the first time, and, later, of *Pride and Prejudice*, *Wuthering Heights* and *Silas Marner*. There were many more, but my favourite was *Jane Eyre*. I doled out the dwindling pages like a miser and when it was finished I would begin it all over again. A handful of those books remained my favourite reading for many more years, even as I read voraciously from anything else that was available. With the first wintry nights and the first fires, out would come *Jane Eyre* again.

Let me stand back for a moment from my entry into that school in 1938, to the moment some time in the nineteen eighties when I realised that my school, like the street from which it took its name, was doomed to fall to the developers. In my day the Dominican College in Eccles Street consisted of five or six handsome Georgian houses, all interconnected, all different in details of plaster and stucco work, whether it might be draped urns, flying cherubs opening roses, or great curling clusters of acanthus leaves. I had thought that it was immortal, that street, and far enough away from the city centre to be of much interest to developers. During all my years there, it had seemed immune to change. Even the changing seasons in Eccles Street, since it was devoid of trees and front gardens, were to be judged only by the quality of the light: the sultry glooms of September when we all walked its paving stones again with a sinking of the heart; the milky fogs or bitter blues of winter; the mysterious clarity of spring light, when you might suddenly see some textual detail leap out at you from a granite plinth, or a single rosy brick, among dozens forming the arch of a coach-house; the thick waspy yellow shafts of June, cutting through alleyways that would shortly be deserted.

We were aware that our street had had a different past, that the great architect Francis Johnston had lived there, he whose spire of Saint George's Church formed the backdrop to our lives, and, of course, worthy old Isaac Butt had lived there, and owned number sixty-four. We were aware too that a member of Grattan's Parliament had lived in sixty-three, Boyle Roche, whose command of the English language was worse than ours, and Cardinal Cullen had lorded it in 1859 but, for longer even than our parents could remember, since 1882 in fact, Eccles Street meant the school and the school meant Eccles

Street. What did schools do in summer? Where did nuns and teachers go? We didn't know and we didn't care. Inevitably, come September, they would be in their appointed places again, and so alas would we be. An end was not envisaged, not even the end of our own schooldays.

But the end of that school was in fact to follow soon after it celebrated its centenary as a place of learning, despite protests by staff and parents and (on preservation grounds) by An Taisce. The Mother General of the Dominican Order is said to have concluded her business with the Mater Hospital and the Archbishop of Dublin during the spring of 1978. They wanted to acquire space for a school of nursing with a 'Catholic ethos' in the street, and to do this they were willing to pay £3,000,000. Neither school staff nor the community of nuns had a hint of the decision to abolish their school until the deal was a *fait accompli*.

When I was at school in Eccles Street, I was very conscious of being part of the city's life, without actually putting that feeling into words. The Municipal Gallery was only a few minutes' walk away and one learned gradually to accept contemporary art as part of the furniture, so to speak. Only another short walk across the Liffey and along by the railings of Trinity College to Dawson Street was the Mansion House, in whose Round Room during the mid-forties Captain (later Lt Colonel) Michael Bowles taught a generation of schoolchildren the meaning of good music. Under his baton I learned to love everything from Handel (*Royal Fireworks* and the *Water Music*) to Schubert. Whether or not we ever learned to *make* music – as those naturally gifted or those whose parents could afford extras with Mairéad Pigóid did – one way or the other, music remained an essential part of our lives.

Theatres in Dublin when I was at school were also on our doorstep. We went in school parties to The Gate and to The Abbey. Shakespeare and Molière irrupted off the printed page and became living theatre for us. These school outings were a special treat, but I can remember doing myself no favour by pointing out to schoolfriends that going to the theatre was nothing new for me. On days when there was a poor house, and the best seats in the Gate were empty, Lord Longford would crook a chubby finger and wave us up where we had no right to be, having paid only a shilling, and that was part of my education too. Art was for everybody, not just for the highest bidder.

However, if you went to Eccles Street at age eleven or twelve, you had to accept that you were an inferior being until you had proved yourself. You were a pleb, a runner-in. The nobility, whether bright or dim, pretty or plain had come right up through the Junior School and so had no taint of inferior schooling about them. In many case their mothers or youngish grandmothers had been Eccles Street girls before them: their Establishment status was absolute. That said, it could be a disadvantage to them in class. Sister Clara, who taught Junior Mathematics, might say, clicking her tongue in disgust: 'Of course, girls, her mother never managed to get over the Pons Asinorum either, or her aunts, for that matter – what can you expect?' To have had a dim mother was not quite as bad having one of unproven social status.

'New' girls even had a whole series of classes to which they belonged up to Intermediate level. They were 'C' classes, whereas girls who had come up through the Junior School were in either 'A' or 'B' as brainpower dictated. When I made it into 'A' level after the Inter exam, I was briefly tempted to scrub out the 'C' stigma on books such as dictionaries and log tables which I would have to use again.

It was not unknown for a new girl to rise above her lowly status by outstanding artistic ability, and this was gauged annually at the 'New Girls' Concert' on Rosary Sunday in October. A beautiful singing voice, an ability to perform Chopin's *Minute Waltz*, or to recite with a fine swagger, 'O, What a Rogue and Peasant Slave Am I' might confer instant status on the lucky performer, and make the large and beautiful oak concert hall rowdy with applause. It was the sort of school that really respected the arts, music in particular. Had not one gawky girl from Mayo won worldwide fame in the nineteen twenties as an operatic soprano? She was nicknamed 'Maggie form Mayo', this girl called Margaret Burke Sheridan, and she haunted choir practice in my day. Maggie would never have played noughts and crosses while waiting for the altos to be brought in, never have left her music at home even if she *had* been a day pupil, never have idled and giggled her way through choir practice. That wasn't how you got to be a world-class operatic soprano, Puccini's favourite Madama Butterfly. (That's as may be. A friend of mine alleges that this could not possibly have been so because he saw photographs of the other 'Butterflies' among Puccini's private collection of memorabilia, and there's not a sight of Maggie among them.)

Margerate Burke-Sheridan's teacher was the illustrious tiny little grey nun called Mother Clement, too old to teach on a regular basis in my time, although she did polish us up for important occasions, such as the 1941 dramatisation of *The Hound of Heaven* by Francis Thompson, which Jimmy Henry from the old Radio Eireann Drama Department directed. The lead was played by a girl from Dundalk called Maura Cranny who had a very beautiful voice and was something of a diva among the Juniors. I never understood the nature of such adoration as she and a handful of others enjoyed until years later when I read Kate O'Brien's *The Land of Spices*.

And that brings me to the strange legend which associates Kate O'Brien with my school. Several of the teachers certainly believed that she had been a boarder around the turn of the nineteenth century. When I met Kate soon after my first book was published I asked her if this was so and if she had ever been banished to the Parlour as I had often been, to report to the Mistress of Studies. She said she rather fancied she never would have been so banished, having been something of a goody-goody at school, but in fact she never was a pupil at Eccles Street. Her school was Laurel Hill in Limerick. And, incidentally, when eventually, some time in the nineteen eighties (Kate being dead by then), I was giving a workshop at that same school, I was astonished to discover that the extremely bright dozen or so girls who sat in front of me knew next to nothing about their illustrious forerunner. One of them came up to me later with a regretful smile. 'Kate O'Brien is not really approved of here,' she said. 'We've never been encouraged to read her.'

'I certainly hope I've encouraged you today', I said, and the helpful girl smiled and nodded as she gathered up her books. The last person to be surprised at that revelation would have been Kate O'Brien herself.

But let's get back to that Parlour! The Mistress of Studies was Sister Enda, who had risen to this eminence from being a boarder of ten or eleven when she arrived in Eccles Street from Kilkenny. I remember her as the immensely tall and powerful Senior English and Irish teacher, in addition to her administrative duties. Her resonant voice could strike terror into the cheeky or delinquent sent to 'see' her in the Parlour. That room where the Georgian ladies had retired to giggle and gossip over their sweetmeats was the place where justice was meted out: 'Go to the Parlour and wait there to see Sister Enda' was an order in which sorely tried young teachers sometimes took refuge. Not too often, though, because their own competence might be called in question.

In the Parlour the smell of lavender wax on the parquet floor had an added pungency, and the sun slanted through liturgical stained-glass windows onto the cheek of the *Madonna della Sedia* by Raphael, full of round-eyed reproach under her turban. You usually waited a long time for Sister Enda, very conscious of the ticking clock on the mantelpiece. The sounds of her arrival were like those of an express train passing a little station, except that unfortunately she would glance into the waiting room, see you, and rattle indignantly to a halt. You would stand up, to be raked for a while in silence by her impatient blue eyes behind the little steely spectacles. She was contemptuous of anybody who wasted anything so valuable as time. In fact, the value she put on time has stayed with me to this day. The Midlands voice was strong and cutting and she could sometimes be a bully but, as I later learned, she had a kind heart and was an exceptionally fine teacher. I remember her habit of linking history and literature together, and the way you were always made conscious of the point where one flowed into the other.

There was a belief among the seniors that she was linked romantically with the revolutionary leader Padraic Pearse and had entered religion after his execution, but of course nobody dared ask her if she and Pearse had even been students together in the National University.

As a Shakespearean interpreter, Sister Enda was memorable, but in my case not so important an influence as my first English teacher, Sister Alvaro, who had enormous round brown eyes under the white wimple and the small breathless voice of an asthmatic. Leaning forward at her desk, she would talk about Shylock, Brutus or Hamlet as though he were somebody she met and conversed with every day, whose every weakness and virtue she knew and understood. The bell always took us by surprise, and Alvaro too. She would frown and look baffled, then gather her books together with the greatest regret.

The senior History teacher was a lay-woman called Margaret Shaw, elderly olive-skinned and brown-eyed, with a collapsing bun of black hair and a well-known passion for Napoleon. We believed she visited his tomb in Paris every summer and left a red rose there. Tout's European history gathered dust in class as she talked compulsively and in detail about Napoleon's genius as a legislator, his young military talents, his Italian and Spanish campaigns, the *Code*

Napoléon, the chaotic condition of Europe when he found it and the Periclean Golden Age in which he might have left it if Wellington and others hadn't got in his way.

My memory is that Miss Shaw may have been a little unsound about 'Le Petit Corporal', but she taught history in splendid sweeping outline, referring you to books only when absolutely necessary, and she didn't mind carrying around what looked like a quarter ton of books from class to class in case anybody might need or demand documentation.

She was also passionately interested in the History of Art and especially in the Renaissance. I found myself thinking of her a few years after I had left school, when Europe was just beginning to pull itself together following the war and I was lucky enough to find myself in Italy. She had taught us to look at well-known pictures as though we had never seen them before, and I did that, especially in Florence, where at the time the battle dust had hardly settled on that magic flower of a city. Botticelli's *Birth of Venus* in the Uffizi not only had the shock of revelation, as though the goddess had only a few moments ago burst from her shell, but it had the more moving shock of recollection, however contradictory that may seem. At fourteen or fifteen I had stuck a blurry photograph of this masterpiece into my history scrapbook and been commended for it by a delighted Miss Shaw. Where was she now? A few years later I instinctively looked around for her at 'Les Invalides' in Paris. There *was* a red rose on the tomb of Napoleon, but no Margaret Shaw in sight.

Lay teachers vanished from our school on a marvellous bonus holiday during our annual *retreat* in late September or early October. During that period of daily Mass, with morning and afternoon lectures in the convent chapel, broken by walks in the Nuns' Garden for the perusal of improving literature (holy books only I regret to say), we were expected to keep silence and, incredibly, we usually did. But the Jesuits among us devised ways of communicating just the same. Written notes (it had been pointed out to us) would be meanly breaking the spirit of the rule of silence, so while walking in twos and threes with open books along the little sun-dappled pathways, we would point out letters of the alphabet to one another and so spell out sentences: 'Is this criminal conversation? Will you cycle home my way today?'

I walked these little paths some twenty years ago when I made a sentimental journey back to our old haunts before the bulldozers moved in to Eccles Street. Inside the school I had been saddened by the feeling of time running out. The smell of polished wood had all but vanished and indeed the corridors seemed dusty. Even the famous Parlour was dismantled and empty. The long winding staircases leading to the Junior School and the kitchens, were full of piled up bric-à-brac ready for departure. Only the bathrooms were gleaming and spotless still, full of Victorian porcelain and brass fittings that would be a collector's delight. The beloved Junior Library was being denuded of books, but I remembered again the minor joys of D.K. Broster, Maurice Walsh and Hugh Walpole, in addition to my real favourites by Charlotte Bronte, Jane Austen, Thomas Hardy and Henry James. Even Henry James himself might have felt at home in the Nuns' Garden which I found still dappled with sunshine, still lovely with rose walks, Victorian garden seats and a little white summerhouse, the sort of garden (in its original state) that is vanishing now from the face of the earth. You can get something of the same feeling of that garden from one of William Leech's paintings, the one of young postulants in white veils walking in procession through a convent garden in Brittany.

I am told that the school itself has not died, but has been given a reincarnation in Drumcondra. I suppose one must be glad, though I have never been tempted to go and see for myself. I can't believe that past pupils of the twenty-first century will have anything so powerful to draw them back as we had to that celebrated street, brushed not only by real history but by the patient ghost of Mr Leopold Bloom, sidling around the corner from Number 7 to purchase his breakfast kidney on that golden and immortal midsummer morning.

The very word 'school' brings me back instantly to Eccles Street, although it wasn't my first experience of being a pupil. My first and unhappy schooling was in Fairview National School, whose ruling sovereign was Miss Batty. She was a substantial lady in her late fifties with thick black 'earphones' of hair and glinting little spectacles. That school was basically an enormous room with desks in the middle and steps at either end, steep wooden steps that could graze the knee of a bare leg. You were allowed to use the desks only for reading and writing and every forty minutes there was a kind of Changing of the Guard ceremony, with Miss Batty at the harmonium playing 'O'Donnell Ábú' and children marching strictly in time either towards or away from the desks. One of the junior staff was detailed to watch out for marchers who wouldn't or couldn't keep time. These children got a smart stroke on the leg with a cane to remind them of their business, and above the bracing rhythms of 'O'Donnell Ábú' you could sometimes hear the odd gasp or yelp of pain. The great Maureen Potter was a pupil at that school, but she was seldom present because of rehearsals and dancing lessons.

I think maybe I have cancelled that school out of memory because my mother angrily removed me from it at the age of eight. That was when I had amused myself one boring day by going over again and again the letter 'C', making it celtic in design, for instance, and then attempting to undo the embellishment. I had finished this particular page of my headline copy before anybody else, hence the boredom. A cruising teacher saw what I had done and said ominously, 'Now I'm going to make an example of you, Madam. Drop that pencil at once and come up to my desk.'

Fifty heads were lifted up joyfully at the promise of entertainment and they got it. The trembling paw was biffed first with two rulers placed one on top of the other, and then with three and then four. After each blow, the teacher watched me carefully (even hopefully, I think) for a sign of tears, but she found none. I was no heroine, but I was bone-stubborn and I was outraged by the extra pain every succeeding ruler inflicted. We had reached six rulers and a hand that was beginning to look like a piece of tenderised steak when the teacher decided she couldn't win this one.

'You haven't even the *grace* to cry, Miss', she gasped at last, and I was sent back to my desk, the hand squeezed under one armpit. Admiring glances cheered me from every corner of the silent classroom. So I was told to put my elbows on the desk and my head resting on my arms and to stay that way with my eyes closed until after school when Miss Batty would be consulted about further punishment. Miss Batty found me in the empty classroom a long time (it seemed to me) after everybody else had clattered away. She made no comment other than to advise me stop out in the yard before going home and let cold water run on my bloated hand. That was my last day in that school, but it has taken more than half a century in Ireland for legislation to be passed making it an offence to beat children in school.

My father cycled to work every day and continued to do so even when most of his colleagues had graduated to modest cars. He told me that he had bought his first bicycle, a Pierce of Wexford, at the end of a year's savings when he got his first job on the Midland and Great Western Railway. The prospects, therefore, of my ever being able to cycle the two or three miles to school via Goose Green and the Drumcondra Road were not great.

Accordingly, when the offer of a bike came from our friends the Irwins, there was no question of refusing, even when I saw the velocipede on offer. It had been sturdily made some time before World War I and now we were well into World War II, which we called The Emergency. This bike had been made with a real lady in mind, a being with her hair in a bun who sat upright and straight-backed on the high saddle, her arms stretched out in front of her and her gloved hands nervously grasping the thin celluloid handle-grips, and if Mrs Copperfield, the child bride, had ever considered cycling, this would have been just the job for her. Her long skirts were protected from the mud by a 'skirt guard', which soon became a trial to me.

The trouble was that the semi-sports model made by Raleigh had arrived in my school and at least fifty of them would be stabled every morning in the bicycle shed. The handlebars were low and gleaming, the spokes of their chrome wheels flashed in the sun, and the people who owned them looked dashing as they turned in by the back lane from Dorset Street. They tended to race showily across the school yard, until they had almost reached their allotted space and then they braked with a series of impressive noises while showering the onlookers with gravel. Girls who rode bikes like that tended to arrive early and stand around in knots afterwards and actually *cheer* my more dignified arrival, to ask if it was much warmer up there where I sat, since hot air ascends. Attempts to maintain classroom status were difficult in such circumstances. Enquiries whether my grannie had died recently, leaving me her old armchair, tended to make me silent with rage, rather than wittily reciprocal. I often wondered if I could lose that excuse for a bicycle, but reason prevailed. There were no bicycle thieves in Dublin at the time, and even if there had been, who would bother to steal mine?

My ascendency even at home did not last long. That first summer when I was the only one of my siblings to have wheels was certainly punctuated by a few occasions when my brother Jim thought my bike worth stealing, leaving me standing at the garden gate with my packet of sandwiches, fuming. The next summer Jim won a scholarship and was allowed to buy a glorious Raleigh sports bike, elegant and fast, like the bikes in school. There I was, still the butt of jokes, envied only by my baby brother Cyril, who was seven years my junior. My mother pointed out that she had never owned a bicycle herself until she was eighteen and I should remember how lucky I was. It didn't help, but the years rolled on anyhow. In time the girls in school found other butts for their wit, and my old bike simply became part of the furniture, no longer worthy of comment. Indeed I remember viewing that upstairs model with a certain amount of affection on the last day of my school life. I had dallied over farewells in the classroom, refused to join the others in the annual orgy at Cafolla's Ice Cream Parlour on O'Connell Street, lingered over futile chat about the English and History exam papers with the relevant teachers, even admitting to one teacher that I didn't really know what I was going to do after school apart from sitting a civil service exam like everybody else. Everybody else seemed to be going on to university anyway, whereas I was not scholarship material, being an imbecile at maths, and so I had no hopes in that direction.

I succeeded in talking myself into a state bordering on melancholy by the time I had reached the bicycle shed and found it empty of everything except my High Nelly which had the chain off. A parting joke on the part of the Raleigh owners? More likely an accident when someone knocked the bike over in her hurry to be rid of school. I had almost finished the revolting job of getting the chain back on again – my hands were covered in oil – when I became aware of being observed from one of the back classroom windows, one of the small rooms (some of which were music rooms) that probably in Victorian times had housed a couple of kitchen maids. Now there was a face framed by its white wimple looking out from the window which was so far away that it wasn't possible to guess which nun it might be. We seemed to be the last two people left in the school, and it has taken me all these years to realise that her thoughts may have been exactly the same as mine. Where do they all go in the summer? What happens to them and what improbable experiences may they not have had before one sees them again in September? Well of course those Septembers when one saw them again were over for ever so far as I was concerned, but the mood remained. I waved in what I hope was a jaunty fashion to the unknown face and then turned to the tap to wash my hands. I realised that this solitary end to my schooldays was in keeping with my life as an only girl, most of whose school friends lived on the other side of the river. My brothers' friends were always within reach.

Eventually I found myself cycling out along the coast road to Red Rock, then a very isolated place close to the heathery slopes of Howth Head. The only houses in Red Rock were a row of coastguard cottages on a slope above the cliff, on the edge of which I threw left my bike and then lay down for a while with eyes half-closed against the brilliant glare of the afternoon sun. The sky was china blue, and the sea was calmly breathing all around me. I might have been the only one person left on this edge of the world. Why hadn't I joined the group of friends who were bound for Cafolla's to drink ice-cream sodas in celebration of school's end? Who knows? I know that 1943 had been a bleak year for me since March when quite shockingly (because my brothers and I had been led to believe she was recovering) my mother had died, indignantly angry at her fate.

One afternoon when I had come in from school to see her, she had hunted away her elder sister who had arrived to look after her and had said to me, maybe believing I was the only one who might understand – and I did: 'You know, Val, I'm not resigned to die as they say because it's not *fair*. I was given a job to do and it's not *finished*. Why am I being taken away from you all? You're children still.'

The speckled blue eyes – speckled my father used to say fondly, like a bird's egg – were angry and resentful, and she didn't even look sick. She looked very young, although she had been gradually losing weight and strength since the operation in January and this was March. I toyed with the daffodils by her bed before bending to kiss her, 'I'm not a child, Mama. I'm eighteen.' At this she smiled, 'God help you, love; it's little you know. It should be the best time of your life and I've spoiled it for you. Bend down to me.' She couldn't lift herself, but she held up a hand and started to wipe the tears off my face with one finger, 'Look after the boys as best you can, won't you? Help Jimmy all you can too. And remember when you're making potato cakes for Jimmy, always put in more potatoes than flour. That way, they won't be soggy. He'll be as lost as any of you. That's why I say it's not *fair*.'

Angry again, she closed her eyes, and my Aunt Eva came in around the bedroom door with another armful of daffodils, 'There, you've tired your mother out. I could have told you. Go on down now to your homework and leave her to me.'

I looked again at my mother's young face before obeying and now, with her eyes closed, she looked already dead. I was halfway down the stairs when I heard a muffled scream such as I had sometimes heard recently in the middle of the night. The last morphine injection was probably wearing off, and it would be an hour before the doctor appeared to give her another. At that time, there seems to have been some creepy collusion between the medical profession and the Catholic church about the amount of morphine it was ethical to give in the case of a terminal illness. Unnecessary suffering, was I think, deemed to be very beneficial to the soul.

All that had been three months before and my father was a totally changed man since her death. His thick auburn hair had gone grey, and (most shocking of all) he had forgotten how to laugh as he learned rapidly how to drink alone. There were no more jokes, no more songs, no more stories. Often he would come home from work and vanish upstairs into his bedroom, not to be seen again until breakfast-time. We had a splendid and handsome brown-eyed old woman called Jenny Kinsella to look after us at this time and she had a fund of stories about the time she had worked as a parlour maid for a doctor in Fitzwilliam Square; clearly she had not moved up in the world when she came to us. She tried one evening to make my father laugh over a thin spidery young man who used to come three days a week as music teacher to the daughter of that house and ended up running away with her mother. Jenny had a genuinely wicked flair for telling such scandalous stories, but you could see that my father was just marking time as politely as he could and waiting for her to go away. No, home was not a cheerful place any more, and cycling out along the coast to Red Rock on that last day of school had been an instinct.

The strange thing about that day was that for the first and only time I accidentally met my brother, Jim, obviously in search of solitude like myself. He arrived on his still gleaming *Raleigh* bike and we had a swim together and loafed around in the sunshine. To my surprise, he ended up choking back his own angry tears and pedalled rapidly away from me. I, on the other hand, seemed to have lost the ability to cry during the weeks and months after 11 March. I had decided to concentrate hard on study, even setting my alarm clock for five o'clock, and working away in the silent house until the sounds of Jenny setting the eight o'clock breakfast came upstairs to me. I would get a good Leaving Cert if it killed me.

I revelled in the hard work because it made me forget everything else and I began seriously to enjoy the set texts, especially the Odes of Horace and the French poetry of Lamartine. Mathew Arnold's 'The Scholar Gypsy' became a particular delight, and learning a great deal of that long poem by heart was no chore. I think maybe this was because in that quiet early morning house it was easy for me to identify with the dreamer, who left his studies and his fellow students behind in Oxford to wander off in pursuit of more ancient wisdom than any seat of learning could provide. In hat of antique shape and cloak of grey, he roamed the Cumner Hills in search of the Romany people who might teach him their ancient lore, but the poem's strong implication is that he never strayed so far from his old life that he could not observe it from a distance while he awaited 'the spark from heaven to fall'. I had a great fellow feeling for that Scholar Gypsy:

> And once, in winter, on the causeway chill
> Where home through flooded fields foot-travellers go,
> Have I not pass'd thee on the wooden bridge,
> In thy cloak and battling with the snow,
> Thy face tow'rd Hinksey and its wintry ridge?
> And thou hast climb'd the hill,
> And gain'd the white brow of the Cumner range;
> Turn'd once to watch, while thick the snowflakes fall,
> The line of festal light in Christ-Church Hall –
> Then sought thy straw in some sequester'd grange.

The Scholar Gypsy was also Mathew Arnold himself in headlong flight from the industrialisation of the time, but I loved the poem anyway, and I sought out some of the landmarks when I spent a weekend in Oxford a few years later with a soulmate who wanted to show off to me his former habitat, New College.

> For most, I know, thou lov'st retired ground!
> Thee at the ferry Oxford riders blithe,
> Returning home on summer-nights, have met
> Crossing the stripling Thames at Bab-lock-hithe
> Trailing in the cool streams thy fingers wet
> As the punt's rope chops round;
> And leaning backward in a pensive dream,
> And fostering in thy lap a heap of flowers
> Pluck'd in shy fields and distant Wychwood bowers,
> Thine eyes resting on the moonlit stream.

Heady romantic stuff that was, the sort that fed the young Yeats years before he gave it an Irish accent and set it back a few thousand years to Fionn and the Fianna and golden Gráinne.

To go, on those brightening early summer mornings from Mathew Arnold to what we shall cautiously call the 'Scottish Play' was a curious shock to the psyche, but I enjoyed that too. Long before Mary Ure in London played Lady Macbeth as a breakable blonde, I liked to imagine her that way, the sort of woman I would run a mile to get away from, but the type most likely to wind up the noble Thane of Cawdor to all sorts of wickedness before cracking up herself.

Well, all that was over now, and I felt adrift for a lot of that summer, not exultant, as were most of my acquaintances who were not going on to any deeper studies than shorthand and typing. It was so gloomy at home that I spent long rainy days reading in the National Library: George Moore, whose *Hail and Farewell* I adored, W.B. Yeats, Lady Gregory's plays and journals, Charlotte Brooke, J.M. Synge, Padraic Colum, and James Joyce whose *Dubliners* set me writing my first short stories, which were awful beyond belief, and whose *Ulysses*, apart from being the funniest book I had ever read, gave me my first and for quite a while my only education in the joyful mysteries of sex.

Long sunny days I spent walking in the Dublin and Wicklow mountains with a small handful of friends, two or three of whom I had been going on hikes with all through our schooldays. To one of those companions I owe my passion for walking. She came from a long line of mountain-walkers. Her whole family had gone up the mountains as soon as they were out of their prams, and in the same way as some people have the nose for a good wine or the instinct to burrow through a mountain of dusty books for auction to find the first edition of *Castle Rackrent* which they *know* is at the bottom, that family had a nose for the right road home, or whatever place away from home they wanted to go.

31

So far as I remember, they didn't use a compass, or even usually a good Ordnance Survey map, although they could read maps as easily as books. Occasionally, as when we climbed Djouce mountain on a day of misleadingly veiled sun and hot winds, they carried a map made for them by their father, who knew every inch of the Dublin and Wicklow mountains as well as he knew his own back garden. He set our course by things like 'the second big rock west of Knockree as you face east from the Glen', and that sort of thing made perfect sense every time to his second daughter, Eileen, who was my friend. At the end of his plotted course, you would see a signpost pointing the way and signifying that a seven-mile tramp east would land you at a place where the last little blue bus from Glendalough would pick you up if you didn't stop once on the way.

It is more than half a lifetime away since I have have seen Eileen, but I am reminded of her every spring whenever I make the first foray into the hills, each time expecting that her inherited mastery of highways and byways will at last prove to have rubbed off on me. It hasn't happened so far. Between relying on Eileen's sense of direction long ago and my own blundering around now with an empty-headed dog, I had a superb guide whom I happen to have married. Maurice Kennedy was the best map-reader I have ever known, and incidentally the best typist and the only person in my experience for whom anything of a mechanical nature was as easy to put together after repair as it had been to pull apart. I have tried without success to follow his advice on the management of mechanical objects. 'If you want to know exactly how something works', he used to tell me, 'just *look* at it.' He sometimes looked at things for hours before he understood them, often making sketches of little nuts and bolts to aid his memory of where they should go, but that, unfortunately, is the sort of *looking* that has always eluded me. 'All you lack is patience,' he used to tell me with a grin, which was a very charitable way of looking at *me*. I often think regretfully of all the things I might have learned from him if only I had listened and taken the trouble. When the respiratory illness which killed him began to take hold seriously some time in the nineteen eighties, he gave me a piece of advice which I had heard first from R.M. Smyllie, the editor of *The Irish Times*, in 1945: 'Go away and come back when you have learned to type.' I thought about this advice and concluded that he was only putting me off. None of the real journalists I knew could type – certainly not M.J. McManus or Ben Kiely or Seamus Kelly. So I went away and I never went back because I never did learn to type, not having any wish (as I saw it then) to end up as a typist.

When the same advice came from the man with whom I had already spent half my life, the same man who as a schoolboy had been taught to type beautifully by his Aunt Jo in Limerick, I didn't really want to recognise it as the advice of a heavy smoker who had used up most of his short lease, and was trying to avoid leaving behind him a wife who typed no better than when he had first lifted aside a slipping ponytail and looked over her shoulder in 1952. 'Here,' he had said, 'give me that page and I'll show you how to set it out.' That's how it began. And a combination of laziness and shame over the difference between one of his beautifully finished pages and mine made me resist his generosity on fewer and fewer occasions. Eventually I stopped resisting, so that I am left now with mounds of typescript bearing his unmistakable stamp of elegance, and a very uneasy conscience about the amount of his life I allowed him to squander on me.

When, in the fullness of time, Donal Foley of *The Irish Times*, gave one of our family exactly the same advice that Smyllie had given to me, I begged her to regard it as serious and she did. Her father was so delighted that he bought her a new typewriter which outlived him.

3

The Open Road

Looking back on an earlier life is a sobering business. If only ... The most useless phrase in the English language. Anyhow, I found myself at the age of nineteen not in the news room of *The Irish Times* but in an office almost next door, in the Department of Social Welfare (Widows and Orphans Branch) as it then was. My job was not just that of a writing assistant but of a grade lower still, known as 'temporary clerical assistant'.

That office housed a strange collection of temporary misfits, including me. Some of them were quite talented and some spoke marvellously fluent Irish, and one equally fluent French. The best of these was a young man with a riotous mop of black curly hair. He came from County Clare and was, I think, a junior executive officer, whatever that was intended to mean. It meant, on reflection, that he didn't belong to my coffee club and that he didn't have to do filing or actually fill in forms for widows and orphans. He and a red-haired friend of his called Leo Houlihan were so keen to share their passionate love for the Irish language that they gave up even fine summer evenings to gather a tableful of youngsters like us around them for *Diaspoireacht agus Caint*. The good thing about this debating society was that you forgot about any deficiency you might have in the matter of your native tongue in order to express your foreboding that the brilliant young Minister for Health,

Dr Noel Browne, would be defeated in his *real* social welfare plans by the Archbishop of Dublin, John Charles McQuaid, and the forces of obscurantism.

The curly-headed founder of our debating society was Mícheál Ó'hAodha and I probably departed from that office before he did to pursue his distinguished career in what was then called Radio Eireann. The reason why I left was not only to get away from the deadly dull and oppressive atmosphere of Dublin at that time, but also because I had sat and passed an examination which removed the 'temporary' part of my status as a clerical assistant – and I could see only too well the danger of *that*. One might actually come to value the permanence of the job and work for promotion and the pension waiting at the end of it. One might grow into a *reliable* guardian of the pink files and never put a single one of them into the wrong dusty cubbyhole when called to the phone. One might (worst horror of all) look speculatively up at the next step in the ladder of rank and start to swot for the exam that would lead to *that*. No, I was getting out. That summer, in a clifftop hotel in Donegal called Port-na-Blagh, I had met a wonderful man called M.J. McManus and his wife Rosie. I was staying there for two weeks with a couple of friends who persisted in wasting their time by sleeping in, so I took to going off by myself for a walk and a swim before breakfast. I can still feel the exhilarating chill of those swims in the dark blue icy waters of Sheephaven Bay, with nobody around except a few redshanks or plunging cormorants in search of their breakfast. It wasn't until I had set off up the cliffs afterwards to a place called The Stallion's Leap that the blood began to flow warmly again in my veins. I still think that the early morning is the best part of any day.

Anyhow, back at the hotel and ravenously hungry by this time, I would usually be reading at our table for fifteen minutes or so before anybody joined me. One morning a tall grey-haired man leaned over from the nearby window table to see what I was reading. We had already exchanged many 'Good Mornings' in the lobby. Now he shook his head and sighed, 'Reading Chekhov before breakfast is good neither for you nor for Chekhov, young lady. Don't do it.'

It sounds ghastly now, but this was pre-Women's Lib., and he was old enough to be my father. The tone was not patronising but familiarly paternal and teasing. He had extraordinarily bright blue eyes, closing and then opening again in the fog of smoke from his cigarette. He lit two more cigarettes, one off the other, before Rosie his wife appeared. Those were the days! I'd break windows if necessary to get away from a smoker now.

By this time we had exchanged names, and Rosie was as friendly and charming as he was. M.J. McManus was literary editor of *The Irish Press*, a paper I hardly ever saw because it was *The Irish Times* which came through the letterbox at home every morning. But it made no difference. My friends filled me in on his widely read and discussed daily feature, called 'This Happened Today', which he published every day for donkeys' years. His passion for history was obvious from nearly everything he said. From that first encounter until the end of the holiday, he always invited one of us to accompany him and Rosie and their friend Chris Fennelly on any drives they might be planning for the afternoon. In the mornings, they played golf. We took to tossing coins to see which of us should accompany the McManuses in their battered little car, because, although we were so much younger than they were, it was always great fun, and the historical lore one picked up was fascinating. It was not true, as M.J. alleged, that I owned a coin which was the same on both sides, but it was probably the only time in my life when I seem to have struck lucky more often than not.

Over that week or so, I got to know M.J. and Rosie well and their marriage – his second – seemed to be as romantic as any courtship. They had been together for about fifteen years at this time, but one day of torrential rain, and the sort of summer hurricane that Donegal so easily produces out of a clear blue sky, he stopped the car a short distance away from the memorial to Lord Leitrim, where we had heard the story of the man's murder in 1878 by a handful of enraged tenants because he had, once too often, exacted the *droit de seigneur* from one of the young women of the townland whose wedding was imminent. We had examined the memorial stone and been very glad to pile back into the car again, drenched to the skin, and here was M.J. pulling up just around the next corner to drag something out of the hedge which didn't appear to come away too easily. He had been drenched all over again by the time he got back bearing a spray of wild woodbine which smelled like heaven. He presented it to Rosie with the remark, 'I just suddenly remembered where this grew – remember the day we found it? That was the day you alleged you'd never heard of Housman: 'Now, of my threescore years and ten, / Twenty will not come again, / And take from seventy springs a score, / It only leaves me fifty more. / And since to look at things in bloom / Fifty springs are little room, / About the woodlands I will go / To see the cherry hung with snow.'

Now this was the late nineteen forties and 'romance' in Ireland was very firmly understood to be confined (if it existed at all) to the period immediately before marriage. No Irish husband in his senses would expose himself to ridicule by scrambling out in the rain to get wild flowers – or any other kind – for his wife, except maybe my own father, but I don't think even he would have done it so publicly. In other words, this was an exceptional man, and so indeed he turned out to be in his generosity (particularly with his precious books) and in his total fidelity to friends and partner alike. One evening when I was working against a deadline on a piece about F.R. Higgins the poet, M.J. offered to lend me an extremely valuable Cuala Press early volume for as long as it was needed.

'You don't mean that I can take it home with me?'

'Certainly. I'll see you home after we've collected it from my house.'

I hesitated only for a second, because I knew the value of the book, but M.J. misunderstood and smiled behind his customary cloud of cigarette smoke, 'As I mentioned', he said carefully, 'Rosie is away for a few days visiting her mother, so you may prefer not to come over to the house, and if so –'

'Of course I'll come'. What did he think I took him for, for heaven's sake?

'I have a daughter not much older than you', he said gently. 'You will be quite safe. I'll see you home on my way back to the office.'

Decorous days, those! But, as I learned, few men in a situation like that would have put their cards so openly on the table.

M.J. remained for the rest of his life a friend of mine, whom I tended to consult about decisions of a serious nature such as how to set about writing a novel, whether or not I ought to throw up my job and go to London, and even about marriage. 'Don't marry an Englishman', he said, when this cropped up a couple of years later. 'He will be just as stupid in bed as in politics.'

'You married an Englishwoman', I said promptly.

'Ah, but that was an entirely different matter. And, by the way there's a young fellow working freelance for us, a young civil servant in the day job, who's also a very fine drama critic. He wants to meet you. He's called Maurice Kennedy – you may have seen his notices from time to time?'

'Are you taking it upon yourself to make a match for me by any chance?'

At this point I was nearer to annoyance than to the laughter I passed it off with, but he set up the introduction anyway, and it became central to my life.

However, as always, I digress. I have left myself staring at a piece of paper which says that I've passed an examination

I never wanted to do anyway. I'm about to be handed down a life sentence in an office, and all I want to do is to escape. But to where? To what? I was qualified for nothing. I had published a few forgettable short stories in little magazines, and a couple of deplorable pieces of verse in the *The Irish Press*. *The Bell*, Sean Ó'Faoláin's famous radical magazine (to which I was first introduced by my father, who always bought it and tossed it across my homework table when he was finished with it) didn't seem to be interested in anything I sent them, until one day I picked out of the crumpled envelope a magic piece of paper which was folded into the rejected manuscript. It said, 'Not these. Send more. Be less subjective.' I first rushed to the dictionary and checked precisely on the definition of 'subjective', and then decided this was the most cheerful communication I had yet taken from one of my own self-addressed envelopes. It might even be Sean Ó'Faoláin's own handwriting telling me to send him more. This wasn't like any other rejection slip. This was *good* news. I turned over again the memo – dark blue lettering on white, the address, 14 Lower O'Connell Street, Dublin, underneath *The Bell* logo. I read the staccato message once again: 'Not these. Send more. Be less subjective.'

This was telling me something with a minimum of words. Certainly objectivity had never been my forte. But *suppose* that advice had been given to the young James Joyce? There wouldn't be any *A Portrait of the Artist as a Young Man*. Maybe quite a lot of *Dubliners*, to be fair.

After a few days, I decided that quarrelling with any advice which came my way from *The Bell* wasn't the way to get published. At the time I'm talking about, workshops and creative writing courses were decades in the future. In the nineteen forties, aspiring writers conducted their own creative writing workshops largely by reading everything they could lay their hands on, and they didn't make such a bad job of it. We were constantly being told (even then) that Irish short-story writers were among the best in the world – and certainly three of them, Ó'Faoláin, Mary Lavin and Frank O'Connor were published far and wide – even in the *New Yorker*, or in an unlikely place like *Esquire*, which paid legendarily high fees.

I suppose if you look back to the creative imperative of the two illustrious Corkmen, you could say that their mentor, Daniel Corkery (who loaned them books and vigorously criticised any pieces of writing they gave him), was the embodiment of a creative writing course, limping around the streets of Cork. When his fledglings took to the air and soared above his head, he didn't much like their performances, but that's another story.

The Bell was founded in 1940 by Sean Ó'Faoláin, and his friend from revolutionary days Peadar O'Donnell found the money to back it. The effect that this little magazine had on the dull and oppressed Ireland of the time was unimaginable. The oppressors were Éamon de Valera and the Roman Catholic Church to whose hierarchy de Valera went scurrying for approval of every new piece of legislation which might offend their Lordships. The famous Constitution of 1937 was drafted bit by bit under the thumb of the arch conservative Archbishop of Dublin, John Charles McQuaid. In his very first editorial Sean Ó'Faoláin gleefully threw down the gauntlet:

> We have to go out nosing for bits of individual veracity hidden in the dust heaps of convention...timidity, traditionalism, wishful thinking. In that search our only advantage is that of being professional writers, publicists and, after a mild and we hope civilised fashion, somewhat unconventional people ourselves. The professional writer's job is for himself (as for others when he turns critic) to be able to sense the synthetic thing a mile away.

That was fighting talk in 1940. And, as you might expect, the editors had to engage in battle over the years with many dinosaurs of the time, among the most vitriolic being Michael Browne, Bishop of Galway, who in 1951 launched an ill-judged attack on *The Bell* which he equated with 'the venom of the *Irish Times* and the Orangemen of Sandy Row'.

> 'Few Catholics', wrote Sean sardonically in the September 1951 issue of *The Bell*, 'who have to consider their careers, not to speak of their wives and children, are going to stray far from Count Mosca's advice to the young cleric: 'Believe what they tell you or not, as you prefer, but never raise an objection. Imagine they are teaching you the rules of whist. And would you raise an objection to the rules of whist?'

> His Lordship speaks bravely of the Church as the Champion of Reason and Liberty. I believe that the universal church is so in a large and generous way ... . But this matter of Catholic writers is the test, could a Graham Greene live here? A Mauriac, a Bernanos, a Péguy, a Mournier, a Pierre Emmanuel? Think of the things that Bernanos said about the Church in his Brazilian Diary! Which, by the way, was partially published by the Jesuit periodical The Month – in England. Can one imagine it appearing in The Irish Monthly?

It seemed to me and my kind – we were in our mid-twenties in 1951 – that we were hearing from this resounding *Bell* exactly what we had been thinking since quite an early age, that the Hierarchical Church Hibernicus was an obscurantist bully which, at the time of Dr Noel Browne and the defeated Mother and Child Bill, shouted for the *right* of good Irish Catholic Parents to provide for their own children themselves – this at a time when there was such abject poverty in the Dublin and rural slums that those very children were dying like flies from preventable illnesses, preventable if one could afford to buy the food to stay healthy or the money to get cured if one fell sick. Of course their Lordships well knew what their real fear was. Social Welfare, which included free health care for mothers and children up to the age of sixteen, might well infringe the repressive sex laws of the Catholic Church. Free medical aid for mothers might well include the provision of effective contraception to reduce the multiple pregnancies for which the poorest women had neither the stamina to endure nor the knowledge to prevent. Families of from twelve to eighteen children often resulted from the carefully maintained ignorance of the poor, who could be (and were) shouted into submission from the pulpits, or had *absolution* withheld from them in the whispering confession boxes.

Anyway, who ever knew where the final push to emigration came from, if hunger didn't dictate it? In my case it wasn't just the prospect of a drab lifetime in the civil service that drove me away. Nor was it the rage one felt against the Church Hibernicus. It wasn't just the dreariness of life at home which was as sudden as a light switched off after the death of my vivacious mother. It was also the pull, strong as gravity it seemed to me then, of the generations for whom taking the emigrant boat was as natural as leaving school and usually without any firmer purpose than to get a perspective on life as we had known it. As for writers, I could hardly think of more than one or two of those I admired who hadn't deliberately gone away as soon as the opportunity arose: George Moore, Wilde, Shaw, Yeats, Joyce, O'Casey, Beckett and away back as far as Congreve and Sheridan.

It so happened that at the end of the nineteen forties inclination and opportunity arrived at the same time. A friend of mine had gone away to teach in Yorkshire on the strength of a very good Leaving Certificate. and she wrote asking me to join her. There were lots of jobs available, she said, and free training after a couple of years if you knew how to go about it.

Within a very short time I was on the mail boat, telling myself I was sailing into exile, silence and cunning and would emerge from them with the novel I had already started to work on in the National Library.

My brother Jim came with me to the North Wall and put my bike on board, a Raleigh only three years old, and the sole fruit of my few years in the civil service. I was extraordinarily proud of that bike, and thought I might even cycle up to my job in Cumberland (I hadn't after all found anything in Yorkshire, which was a pity because I rather fancied myself striding across the moors like Emily Brontë). After hugging my brother, who extracted a promise from me to come home for Christmas, before he got lost among the crowds, that siren on the old mailboat seemed to me, as we pulled away from the North Wall, the loneliest sound in the world, and those people waving on every side of me were surely the drabbest and saddest lot I could have chosen to join. But there I stood among them watching the lights of Dublin growing smaller and blurrier behind us and vanishing at last into the marine mists of September.

'Come on down girl, and have a jar with us', a fellow countryman at my elbow said. 'Take your mind off things, like.' I said thanks but no thanks and moved away from the kind southern voice. The sounds coming up to me were already loud and boozy and I would have liked nothing less than to be caught up on that tide. Drink I associated with loneliness rather than with good company, or if not loneliness, like my father's, then truculence like one of my favourite uncles when he would drop in on us after a bad day at the races. One look at his inflamed face and you knew he had not backed a winner but had gambled too much on the same couple of losers. So there would be no jokes, no thrilling flights towards the ceiling from his swinging arms, no fun. Failure to borrow from either of my parents, who usually had a good use for every penny, would result in an ugly curl of his lip that made Frank look like somebody else.

43

He would fling himself down on the old couch after refusing to share our meal and would be snoring loudly in a matter of minutes. Attempts to get him up to the spare bedroom were usually futile and he would be found still snoring when we all trooped down to breakfast the next morning. He was the best-looking and the only artistic one among the uncles, but he had been thrown out of art school for idleness and then suddenly got married to a partner as flighty as himself. Their small twins were cared for among the family when both parents escaped to the races, sometimes even to a country race-meeting from which nobody knew when they might return.

I liked Frank when he was sober, but I didn't like him as much as the regular Saturday night visitors, Bobby and Mick, who were old friends of my father's and who adored my mother. Sometimes Mick would manage to find for her a small box of Black Magic chocolates – extremely scarce in the early days of the Emergency before they were withdrawn altogether by the makers, who said they preferred to do that rather than lower the standard of the product. I would sometimes be rewarded for my wickedness and allowed down for a chocolate from my hiding place at the bend of the stairs. You see Mick was my godfather and, even after I had finished my chocolate, I would be allowed to join the party around the fire if he happened to be in a musical mood, which was very often. I can't have been more than ten or eleven when Mick died, but I can call up before me now every detail of his appearance. He was a dark, stocky man in his good navy-blue suit and he had bushy black hair and eyes partially concealed by thick black eyebrows. The lower part of his face was hairy too. He had, like my grandfather, a moustache of the kind known as 'Piccadilly Weepers', which tended to be abrasive when he kissed you and to be troublesome when he drank his tea. On Saturday nights he did not drink tea. On Saturday nights he would gaze affectionately at the bottle of stout my father had poured for him, relishing it even before the first mouthful, his blue eyes as happy as a child's.

The important thing about Mick was that he was an engine driver for the Midland and Great Western Railway. He had that magical job, which my brothers (and every one of their friends who heard how Mick made his living) wanted to be when they grew up. You wouldn't guess what Mick's job might be when he came to us direct from the Gaiety Theatre on Saturday nights. He was an engine driver by trade, but an orchestral conductor by aspiration, and the Dublin Grand Opera Society's season was his big time. He knew by heart the scores of his favourite operas, all by Wagner: *Tannhauser*, *Lohengrin* and *The Flying Dutchman*. Mick could imitate the various instruments of the orchestra, and he often gave us a potted version of the opera he had seen. I can still picture him standing before his dream orchestra in his square-toed, glossy black boots; can still see a finger of his big hairy hand delicately bringing in a solo clarinet or a shimmer of the concert harp. He would occasionally interrupt himself to show you how a Carl Rosa version differed from the performance he had just attended. He had a fine baritone voice and could give you the odd aria if he was in the mood.

Mick's passionate enthusiasm for opera was taken for granted at home, although my father didn't share it. He was a drama man himself, but Mick belonged to a depleted inner circle of friends who had all grown up together and he was welcome to bring his orchestra into our kitchen whenever he pleased. My mother indulged him too and often on week nights she told me stories from the operas, about which Mick had made me curious. Her own taste ran to musical shows like *No, No, Nanette* or *The Student Prince*, but she had great admiration for Mick's talents and I often heard her saying that if he'd had the benefit of a musical education, he might have become a conductor or even a composer. He had picked up such knowledge as he had from the gods of the Gaiety Theatre. That was the place, my father said, where you often heard better voices at the interval than during the

45

performance because that was where the real cognoscenti were, Mick among them.

One winter when I was about ten and suffering from book starvation (having read everything in the house), Mick went missing from those Saturday nights at home, but coming up to Christmas he sent me a large brown paper parcel. I felt it carefully around the edges and decided it must be a big book, maybe *Fairy Tales of the British Isles* or a compendium of the Katy books by Susan Coolidge or even – the crazy idea occurred to me because Mick had mentioned it once – maybe an Illustrated Children's Encyclopaedia which I coveted. I refused to open the parcel until I got home from school, preferring to tease my brain about the possible nature of the book. It was raining that day, the sleety rain of those last days before the Christmas holidays, and my mother took my coat to shake it out in the hall. She reminded me that I had two friends coming to tea and I should open Mick's parcel in case it might contain something to eat, which I could share with them. I laughed at this bizarre idea but she was right. It was not a Children's Encyclopaedia which would last for hundreds of readings or more, not a collection of Katy books, not the *Fairy Tales of the British Isles*, but it was indeed something we could share: a big box of those sumptuous chocolates which used to be called Whipped Cream Walnuts and which in those days had a whole walnut in the bottom as well as on the top.

On top of the box was a glossy sepia postcard from Mick saying he wished me everything I wished myself (this when he *knew* I wished for books every time) and he was sorry he wouldn't be over to see us until the New Year. His handwriting was of the flawless copperplate style taught to children in the old primary schools. I was never so disappointed by anything before or since in my whole life, and I can even remember how badly I behaved and how the evening ended (when the door closed behind my departing friends) with my being sent up early to bed.

'Spoiled', my mother said sadly. 'A spoiled ungrateful girl, and Mick must have sent his sister out to buy that present because he couldn't leave his bed himself.' It was the mid nineteen thirties. If you didn't contract tuberculosis from contaminated library books, you might catch pneumonia from playing out of doors with no coat on, which was just as bad. The sulpha drugs had only just been discovered and antibiotics were still well into the future. Pneumonia was often fatal even if you were wrapped up like an Egyptian mummy in thermogene wadding and left behind drawn curtains in a warm room until the *crisis* – whatever that was – had come and gone.

Mick was not kept in his warm room. His sister took fright and rushed him off to the Mater Hospital where he died a few days after Christmas. He was the only person I have ever known who carried a whole symphony orchestra around with him in his head.

Bobby was the other Saturday night guest and he wasn't such fun. He was one of my father's numerous politically minded friends and he couldn't understand why Éamon de Valera stubbornly refused to help Britain in her fight against fascism. What had the so-called seven hundred years of 'persecuting' *us* got to do with the fact that the Nazis were even now rounding up Jews and Gypsies and other persecuted minorities and keeping them like cattle in pens until the time seemed right to deal with them? The British and the Allies were the only hope for a future that those innocent people had, and Ireland ought to be out there lending a hand to overthrow this madman called Adolf Hitler.

'All that is John Bull's propaganda', my father said uneasily. 'John Bull has always been an accomplished liar. He lied about what orders he gave the Black and Tan thugs when he dispatched them over here. He forged the Parnell papers. I for one wouldn't believe a word that passes the lips of Mr Winston Churchill.'

'It's the truth for all that.' Bobby had the tired voice of

somebody who probably lived with a good deal of pain. He was lame in one leg, and he had a peculiar way of holding his shoulders as though one were heavier than the other. Some family business whose nature I have forgotten was managed by his elder brothers and they were regarded as quite wealthy people. I remember that when Bobby died, and it was a grievous sin, according to Archbishop Charles McQuaid for Roman Catholics to put a foot inside a Protestant church while divine service was in progress, we were all marshalled proudly by my father to attend his old friend's memorial service. Up to then, I had never known or cared what faith Bobby espoused. Because he had a lot of spare time on his hands, he made a hobby of woodwork, and the first desk I ever sat down to write at was a birthday present Bobby made for me when I was eleven or twelve. He had been dead for a couple of years before the horrors of the Nazi death camps became generally known – initially to us through the dispatches of Denis Johnston, who was war correspondent for the BBC at the time. I can remember my father's silence and the way he shook his head over the first horrifying stories. 'God be good to you, Bobbie,' he said. 'I should have listened to you. I'd be the first to shake your hand and apologise now if I could.'

Why I should have remembered those two dead friends of my father's with such vividness on that first of many night-sailings away from home, I don't know. That old life of my childhood had died with my mother, leaving behind a beached shell that was not quite my father. And I believed I had cast off that former life like a snakeskin and that I would never think about it again. My sights were elsewhere, and yet on that night I was not going forward into the future but back into childhood, sitting at the bend of the stairs on my reluctant way up to bed, listening to the laughter and the half-understood conversations in the kitchen, wondering how many hours after midnight those old friends of my father's would break up and go home – Mick and Bobbie, and another Saturday guest I suddenly remembered called Douglas Stewart, who would walk all the way across the sleeping city to his home called Malakoff House on the Rathgar Road. He was a Greek scholar who would remember my birthday with gifts of books and cards, always wishing me 'Many happy anniversaries of 14 February. There can be no returns, happy or otherwise, my dear girl. Time past is just that. Gone.'

Time past was all around me, all the same, on that night-sailing which I spent mostly alone up on deck, watching the incredible whiteness of the churned foam, listening to the happy drunks on the lower deck, and trying to make out a dim star or two in a particularly dark sky. I stayed up there until some sort of balance had returned. I was free. I had a half-written novel in my suitcase. Time past, as Douglas had said, is just that. Gone. Time to move on.

4

Carlisle

At a quarter to eight every morning Mrs Petteril put breakfast on the table whether anybody was present or not. She was a neatly turned out and fast-moving Scottish lady with wavy dark hair and a rosy face which might have been very pleasant had she ever smiled. I never saw her smiling during the twelve months I spent with Liz McConville from Belfast in that handsome Victorian house in Carlisle.

The dining room had a bay window that faced towards Scotland, so it was never visited by the morning sun. The only light came from the well-polished old silver on the sideboard. The curtains were held back by brass ties and between them was a dangerously healthy-looking rubber plant. Was it my overworked imagination or did that plant creep a little closer to the dining table every day, with the eventual purpose of sharing our toast?

There were two kinds of lodger in Mrs Petteril's – the 'cooked breakfast' elite, and those others like us, usually young and always hungry, who could only afford the other sort. A 'cooked breakfast', as I recall it, was not quite the bacon and eggs variety as at home because in 1948 the war had been over for only three years and there seemed to be generally much less food on offer than there was in Dublin. Mr Misstear, who worked in the bank and who sat opposite me across the large mahogany table, had as strange a collection of cooked things on his breakfast plate as you could possibly imagine. Nutty gizzards there must have been and maybe even fried hencod's roes. Not much liver that I could see but certainly fried bread, and half a tomato and something like a potato cake. Mrs Petteril would give a sort of bob curtsey as she left this aromatic platter in front of Mr Misstear and threw over her shoulder at us a terse assertion, rather than an enquiry, that we must be all right for toast. After our bowls of porridge there were two slices of toast each every morning in the beautiful silver toast rack and sometimes an odd one which we carefully cut in half. There was never enough butter or marmalade left for that extra half, but if Mr Misstear was in a hurry for work, he would gobble up his nutty gizzards and not bother with his toast and marmalade.

Those were feast days for Liz and me, but unfortunately we couldn't delay and properly enjoy the windfall because Mrs Petteril might be back at any moment to clear away the dishes, and on one occasion when she found us munching and murmuring over our good fortune, she stopped indignantly in the middle of the room and stared at us, for what seemed like ten minutes, before remarking that up to this she hadn't taken any Irish into her house and that we were the first. Liz had the presence of mind to smile and jump up to open the door for her when Mrs Petteril had loaded up the silver tray. She was rewarded with a nod.

There wasn't much to laugh about in Carlisle. It was a dour town whose best assets were its ancient rose-red walls and its proximity to Scotland and the Lake District.

What I remember best about Carlisle is cycling away on free days during that long Indian summer, and swimming with Liz in the Solway Firth or lazing on as sleepy a little beach as ever you would find at that time in the West of Ireland. It was horrifying some years later when I had children of my own to learn that people didn't swim in those quiet little places

51

any more because of Windscale, now known as Sellafield. Not even that *name* was known to anybody I knew in the late nineteen forties. The pretty Cumbrian coastline had not lost its innocence then. Sheep could safely graze in the surrounding hills. Small children could build sandcastles and wade out into the warm shallows with shouts to their mothers to look at them. There were no fears of leukemia or brain tumours for them, no horrendous forebodings that the pigtailed little girls with dresses tucked into their knickers might at some future time give birth to brain-damaged or mutilated babies. The worst danger anybody knew was war, and that was over.

I hadn't expected to find English people so friendly and easy-going. Travellers' tales of returning emigrants spoke of long silent train journeys where, in cramped carriages, men erected their barriers of newspapers and women gazed unblinking out of the carriage windows for fear of catching somebody's eye. You could travel a hundred miles without hearing the sound of a human voice other than 'Tickets, please', the returning travellers said. I found these stories greatly exaggerated, I must admit, but, come to think of it, an incident in the spring of the following year can't quite be forgotten.

On a showery March Saturday I was out cycling by myself along the border-lands between England and Scotland, enjoying the fresh air and the cold breeze and even the clouds scudding along before the north wind. There was already growth in the air, a mist of green among the upper branches of the larches. I fell into chat with a man whose long white farmhouse stood just a bit up the hillside from us. I was leaning on the handlebars of my bicycle and he on his slash hook – he had been thinning hedges. He had asked me what crops you'd find growing in the West of Ireland, where his wife had a second cousin. He had often wondered what sort of life that man could live on thirty acres – would he be a prosperous lad or not? It was quite hard to convince my companion that somebody born and bred in Dublin wouldn't necessarily know the details of farming lives, which we encountered only occasionally during holidays. He nodded and said he had never taken a holiday in his life and wouldn't know what to do with himself if he ever did. He was as chatty as anybody at home would be until the heavy clouds seemed to stop and unload their burden right above our heads. The farmer then bade me a courteous farewell and went off at a gallop to his nearby house, leaving me to drown in the downpour by the side of the road. I don't believe there was any malice in it. Simply, I had my place in the landscape and he had his. But it would be hard to imagine any farmhouse or even any one-roomed cottage in the West of Ireland where you wouldn't be urged to come in out of the rain.

The convent school where I taught English was almost exactly the same as such a school would be at home. At Assembly and morning prayers, a little Principal with a starched coife and the hint of a hot potato in her mouth would comment on any misdemeanour of the day before. Offending pupils would be warned anonymously that unless they owned up after school, their names would be announced the next morning. I remember one occasion when the Principal's voice shook with emotion over the unmentionable thing that a pupil had done. Gone into the nearby woods with the gardener, we wondered? Embezzled money meant for school books? Murdered one of the prefects, a couple of whom would make this a very understandable act of self-defence? None of these, in fact. The criminal in question had attempted to flush away a sanitary towel in the lavatory, a giggling colleague told us at break in the staff room, and it was this which had accounted for the humiliation of the whole convent when a plumber had to be called in.

Listening to the shocked Principal, I had found it impossible to decide what the terrible act might be which had caused her such upset. The girls seemed to me a great deal more biddable than I remembered *we* were at their age at home.

53

I remembered with shame, even at that remove, how we as third years had systematically tormented a young French graduate whose father was a District Justice, but whose own grasp of discipline was not great. She was said to be very clever and we were her first students. She stood aghast before us in her graduate's cap and gown as a rising tide of mirth came up from the back row. She had very large dark eyes and a mouth that turned down at the corners. Her cheeks were a mottled scarlet and her method of dealing with the noise was to murmur 'Please, girls' four or five times in rapid succession while literally wringing her little chilblained hands. On one memorable occasion the Mistress of Studies (she of The Parlour) alerted by the noise, thundered into the classroom, told our despairing teacher to take a break, which she did at once, departing in tears, and then read the Riot Act to us before settling down to give us a most inspiring lesson on French poetry, concentrating on Lamartine. *Dieu que le son du cor est triste au fond des bois* comes back thrillingly to me across six decades.

At the end of the lesson she spoke severely to us, but quietly this time: 'Now let me explain why there will be no break for any of you today and why barbaric behaviour of this kind will simply not be tolerated in Dominican College.' Shocked at the cutting of our break, we listened in silence, and heard about the generosity of spirit necessary to make allowance for the inexperience of a brilliant young scholar who had distinguished herself at university, in Ireland and at the Sorbonne, and would mature into the finest of teachers if treated in a civilised manner. It was the second time in my life that I had been brought face to face with the difficulties some teachers experienced. We thought that all the difficulties were on *our* side of the fence. The first time was in primary school when, after a particularly gruelling session with a tweedy inspector from the Department of Education – who, we mistakenly believed, had come to examine *us*, our teacher saw him politely to the school gates and walked back into the classroom in torrents of tears. We liked her, and couldn't understand. We were actually shocked into silence.

My own experience with the only inspector I ever encountered was different, but just as punishing in the end. It was towards the end of the school year and I was trying to decide whether I should come back in September or not. Teaching didn't really leave a lot of time for anything else although I enjoyed it. Anyhow, I wasn't bothered one way or the other about the visit of the inspector. I was told that by the Principal that he usually selected his own classes to walk in on, with no introduction, and I should just proceed with my lesson as usual. I had actually forgotten about a possible interruption, and in 4A we were well into how Mark Antony's funeral oration differed so radically from that of Brutus and why (in the circumstances) his approach was better, when a short, sandy-haired man entered the classroom after a brief knock at the door. The children stood up in some dismay and he waved them back to their seats before he introduced himself to me with a quite pleasant smile. His accent was strongly Scottish.

'I've been given permission', he said, after we shook hands, 'to make a nuisance of myself by just sitting in at the back of your class. You must forget about me altogether.'

'Certainly', I agreed, and proceeded to attempt to do just that. In fact, he was so unobtrusive that, with a bit of initial effort, it was quite easy to forget about him because the class followed my low-key response as we got on with discussing the skilful way Mark Antony played with the emotions of the mob during his funeral oration over the body of his friend, Julius Caesar. When I asked for an example of this, the sharpest girl gave us one and effortlessly quoted:

You all do know this mantle; I remember
The first time ever Caesar put it on:
`Twas on a summer's evening, in his tent,
That day he overcame the Nervii.

55

She continued for another couple of lines until I asked the class could they remember an example of the approach Brutus took, which was so different. There was no stopping the class once they got going. Relevant quotes came flying from all directions and it appeared that these girls had forgotten the presence of the inspector or else had decided to enjoy themselves by showing off. About five minutes before the bell was due to ring for break, the little man came up through the ranks, briefly complimented the girls, shook hands with me again as the bell clanged and said with a really charming smile, 'That's the first English lesson that's ever interested *me* for many a long day. My compliments to you, Madam.'

The visit of the inspector wasn't mentioned again until into the summer term. I had decided to stay on for another year and get better acquainted with Scotland during free weekends. The last thing I expected was the sack. The Principal was clearly more than a bit embarrassed as she told me the reason. It seems the inspector had been shocked to learn that I was teaching a Junior Certificate class with no formal academic qualifications. Such assistant teachers as me were being weeded out of the system, he told her, and unfortunately would have to be let go if the government grant was to be continued. She was particularly sorry to lose me for the girls' sake and my results in the previous year's Junior Certificate had been outstanding, blah, blah, blah.

In fact, such is the resilience of a twenty-three-year-old that I didn't care. My sights were set elsewhere anyhow, but for the moment I needed a job. An ad in *The Times Educational Supplement* brought in twenty-one replies and, after travelling to six or seven interviews, I made my choice of a finishing school set deep among the woods of Hertfordshire, an Elizabethan manor house whose beauty delighted me. I had taken the precaution to enrol myself as an extramural Arts student at London University for the following autumn, and when I stepped off the train in smoky Carlisle on the evening of the successful interview, I was so buoyantly happy that the thought of parting with my old comrade Liz hadn't even occurred to me.

We were making illegal coffee down in Mrs Petteril's kitchen – it was one of her bridge nights – when the thought occurred to Liz and me together. Why not come with me? I had described the beechwoods, the formal gardens, the incredible beauty of the ancient house. Liz took a deep breath and said she would write for permission from her parents that very night, which she did. Her father wrote back promptly saying no, and she never questioned his decision. The parents, it seemed, didn't want her to move away from the safe domain of a convent school. I pondered the difference between us as I penned a note to my father giving him the news and my future address. He wrote back wishing me luck and enclosing a fiver. Let the luck go to my novel, I said to myself. I had finished the first draft in April, and revised it, with a lot of help from Liz's typewriter, but I would miss her company even more than her typing, I assured her.

Meanwhile, before the end of term, there was the Lake District to explore at weekends and long meandering walks over the moors following what remained of Hadrian's Wall. Moreover, the untouched summer awaited me in Ireland, and a planned cycling holiday along the coast from Kerry to Mayo, during which a miraculous sun burned on from dawn to dusk every day. But, best of all, I met in person an icon of my schooldays.

5

Face to Face with
Kate O'Brien

Twenty-four hours after a spell of torrential rain, I arrived in Roundstone one late afternoon, having cycled that most delightful stretch of bogland from Clifden. Bog cotton seemed to have sprung up everywhere, like unseasonable snow, the result I suppose of hot sun after rain. The little fishing village was golden in the evening light, and the waters of the bay were as blue as the Mediterranean. It was tea-time.

This was the era in rural Ireland when you could have anything you liked for tea so long as it was rashers and eggs. You would have had dinner at 'dinner time', which was one o'clock. Everybody in Roundstone seemed to be indoors having tea. The homely smell of frying bacon hung over the village, and the dogs drowsed on in the afternoon heat. Two barefooted little boys were perched up and swinging their legs on the harbour wall opposite O'Dowd's pub. They were sucking an ice cream which they passed one to another. I went in to O'Dowds and asked the curate if they could put me up for the night. He said, so far as he knew, they were booked up by a party of anglers from England, but that the Miss McGlynns could surely fit me in. Mrs O'Dowd came out from behind the counter, wiping her hands on her apron. She stood with me on the pavement as she pointed up the hill which wound along the bay. 'They live in the second of two houses up there on your left-hand side. They'll know how to look after you right enough.'

I thanked her, and because I preferred to walk up the hill rather than cycle in the heat, she told me to leave my bike outside the pub and she would keep an eye on it (not that any piece of property would be in any danger in any country village at that time in Ireland).

I found the two McGlynn ladies in their pretty house at the monastery end of the village and they couldn't have been more hospitable. They cooked me bacon and eggs and produced some wonderful brown bread straight from the oven to go with it. Then they advised me where to swim and what to see in the village, including Kate O'Brien's house just across from the harbour. '*The* Kate O'Brien?' I asked. Oh yes, *the* Kate O'Brien, who had lived among them for quite a while in that lovely house beyond there. They showed it to me. They were as proud as though a bishop or a film star had come to live in their village. To my amazement, they spoke of this superb writer as though she were a prized heritage possession, which indeed she was. You have to remember that Kate O'Brien had been banned by the notorious Censorship of Publications Board of de Valera's Ireland, so most godly people of the time would not have boasted of her presence among them. My kind hostess pointed across the glimmering blue water to where Kate O'Brien's house stood square and white under the circle of Paul Henry mountains. It was called 'The Fort'. I would, I said, take a stroll across and look at it.

'Why wouldn't you knock at her door and say hello?' the younger sister urged me. 'Miss O'Brien wouldn't mind at all, and you a writer like herself?'

I knew only too well that I wasn't a writer like herself, and that, if I lived to be twice as old as my twenty-five years and worked all the time, I was unlikely even then to end up a writer like herself. But I remembered the younger sister's eager face – eager to share one of the sights of Roundstone with a visitor – as I stood looking at the beautiful house in the golden light welling up from the water all around me. It was an imposing house, and I knew, by repute, that she was an imposing woman, jealous of her privacy (as any writer should be) and impatient above all else with bad manners, which a call out of the blue by a stranger might well be termed.

I was conscious, too, of being dressed still in those old cycling shorts, with scratched brown legs, dusty sandals, and my hair salty and tousled from the swim. With a little effort, I could have made myself more presentable but I hadn't intended to call, so I couldn't possibly knock at the door now. Could I? I'm not, at the best of times, a great dropper-in. I don't like taking friends by surprise and especially writers who may well be working. I'll never know what exactly compelled me to knock at that particular hall door despite all the reasons why I should not, but I did know that if I went away now, I would regret it.

There was hardly a pause between my knock and her appearance. Kate O'Brien looked with amusement out of the wonderful smoke-blue eyes at my untidy long hair and well-worn sandals and I think that even if I hadn't mumbled my name, she might still have asked me in to find out what had brought this apparition to her doorstep. I remember thinking that she wasn't a forbidding person at all, but a woman who seemed to have a vital curiosity at her core, who sometimes at least was content to have cherished routines broken for the sake of whatever diversion the unexpected might bring. When she heard my name, she shook my hand with the most kindly warmth and invited me in and I don't think any recognition before or since has ever given me greater pleasure. She said she hadn't read my novel yet but had ordered it the week before in Galway. 'Come on in', she urged me.

Her study to the left of the hall door was full of books and marine light, a large and beautiful room with a littered desk under one of the windows and a seal-point Siamese cat staring from the mantelpiece. The cat in her beauty and stillness might well have been carved from Parian marble, with turquoise stones for eyes, but she proved she was not by getting up and strolling long-legged among the other ornaments, sitting for a moment on a heavy gilt clock before taking up her position at the far end of the mantelpiece where the late sun lit her theatrically. When I had admired her and stroked her, Kate O'Brien said she liked to show off before visitors and always chose her place carefully to suit the time of day.

The other thing I remember clearly about that peaceful and friendly room is the portrait of a beautiful young woman in a green dress above the desk. Her long neck and slender bare arms somehow echoed the pose of the cat. Was the painter Orpen? Anyhow, this was the young Kate around about the time of her marriage in London, when her play *Distinguished Villa* had a long run in the West End. Comparing this lovely creature with the heavy but still handsome woman beside me was inevitable, and she noted it with a shrug as she handed me a glass of wine. Only the smoky blue, ironic eyes were the same.

What did we talk about? First, she politely made me talk about my novel, what plans I had to follow it quickly with another. This, she said, was important. She told me about her own days in London when I mentioned I was working there, and she made one smiling reference to a brief, not happy, marriage. And then, at some stage, she said something so strange and so significant – of this my memory is quite clear – that I didn't know what to say that wouldn't sound trite or foolish or vulgarly inquisitive. She said, 'I never wanted to be a mother, you know. I'd have liked to be a father'. I admit with some reluctance that I knew of homosexuality because of Oscar Wilde, but stupidly I hadn't really associated it with women. The deep and beautiful masculine voice made her statement seem entirely natural, somehow, though not in relation to the girl in the green dress above us on the wall.

We drifted into talk about work. She swore she was lazy, willing to do anything but sit down before the empty page. Yet all those brooding and wonderful novels on which I had grown up? She brushed them away impatiently. The only one she cared about was *The Ante-Room* and that had been written a long time ago and was now out of print. Her publisher was fed up with her – she didn't work half hard enough. I talked of my own favourite *The Land of Spices* and expressed my determination to get at *The Ante-Room* in the National Library before going back to London. At this Kate got up and began to rummage around her bookshelves. No, alas, she had indeed nothing but her file copy of *The Ante-Room*.

We began to talk about Professor Magennis and his demented Censorship of Publications Board and I remembered that *The Land of Spices* had been banned as being 'in its general tendency indecent' because of one decorous sentence about a girl's homosexual father. She laughed heartily at the idea of that grave study of a nun's spiritual odyssey 'being in its general tendency indecent' and she quoted what Seán O'Faoláin had said about the reason for its banning. Too ignorant to know the George Herbert poem from which the title came, the gentlemen of the Censorship of Publications Board had equated the land of spices with 'something spicy' and so had given it the hammer. She seemed genuinely more amused than bitter, and I told her that I had half-hoped my own book would be banned and so catapult me painlessly into the company of my betters. She shook her head and said it was a matter of income. It had halved hers, at least, for that and the following year.

It was dusky but with the sea still glimmering all around us when I took my leave of her at last. I told her I was pushing off next morning after a swim, but she insisted that I must see her local and have a farewell drink with her. That is how I learned of her secure place in that little community. 'Miss O'Brien' had a word for everybody in the steep cobble stoned street and in the low-ceilinged little pub which was also the general store of the village. Everybody also had a bit of news or chat for her. She bought sweets for a small gaggle of local children and asked me if ever anywhere I had seen a more wonderfully beautiful lot. Before I cycled off, she pulled out of her pocket a Penguin edition of *Pray for the Wanderer* inscribed 'For Val Mulkerns to remind her of Roundstone, September 1951' – as though I could ever forget, and touching that yellowed volume now I am warmed all over again by her extraordinary kindness. We would, we agreed, meet again some time when she was in London, but I thought she would probably forget. She did not forget.

Somehow in London, however, it was different. Over lunch in *La Belle Etoile* in Soho, I saw the side of Kate that did not suffer fools gladly. I made a foolish remark about Venice, one of the places she regarded as sacrosanct. She forgave me over the course of the meal but I don't think she ever forgot. I was proud and poor and living at that time on thirty pounds a month when you really needed forty pounds, so of course nothing would do me but to invite her over to dinner to meet a few friends at my flat in Bayswater. She smiled her thanks very graciously but said she could never eat dinner these days and had given up trying. I took it from her evasion that she imagined a terrible meal assembled from tins, and I was mortally offended, having recently learned to do wonders with a slow-cooking steak casserole using plenty of garlic and a splash of wine. Also, I felt she imagined bohemian squalor, whereas I put most of my money into what I took to be gracious living. I lived alone because I was a prig and could never abide the mess created by other people. Anyhow, there was a slight hiatus in the friendship, although we exchanged a few letters and when I quarrelled with my publisher she was kindness itself, worrying that a recommendation from her to Heinemann might do me more harm than good since they were so annoyed with her for dragging her heels over *The Flower of May*.

'Very soon', she wrote, 'we'll talk things over in Dublin. I'm half-dead with the book and all sorts of annoyances.' That was late summer 1952 and I was by then working in Dublin with Peadar O'Donnell on *The Bell*. I got married the following year and lost touch with Kate for a while, but eventually in October 1953, *The Flower of May* arrived for review on my desk, sent across the road by Mervyn Wall from what was then Radio Eireann in Henry Street. I read it eagerly, remembering how troublesome it had been in the making. Nothing of this is obvious from the text, and although I wouldn't count it among the best of her novels, I found it moving, though perhaps a little too soft and elegiac. It was a return to the romantic mood of *Mary Lavelle*, and Giraudoux's phrase occurred to me: 'Je connais les jeunes filles et leur intransigence.' Kate's civil response from Roundstone was immediate:

> 'I am most truly grateful. Clearly you have understood the book and praised it generously and with precision. Where do you live now? Where does one find you?'

Writing at this remove, I think that the people who linger most insistently in the memory are people one hasn't known quite well enough. Kate for me for ever falls into this category. I was reminded of her again some years after her death when an elderly neighbour who had been ill and whom I visited, started to talk spontaneously one day about a family she knew around the end of the nineteenth century in Limerick; she thought they were the children of a vet in Mulgrave Street, or 'anyhow he had something to do with horses'. Her sisters knew the elder boys and girls better, she said, and used to attend dances and tennis parties at their house, but the one she knew and liked best was Kate, the youngest, the flower of that particular flock in her opinion.

'Not Kate O'Brien?' I asked, and the old lady nodded and asked me if I had family connections in Limerick. I told her no, but I knew and loved Kate's books, and that the elderly Kate had been a good friend.

'Oh', the old lady said in surprise, 'so she wrote books too!'

6

How Not To Dine
at the Cafe Royal

It was no wonder therefore that the second embarkation into exile seemed lonelier than the first. I carried a bare and elemental and distractingly beautiful West of Ireland landscape away with me in my head, a place haunted by the ghost of John Millington Synge who had made it familiar to me long before I ever saw the West. And now there was the living and welcoming presence of Kate O'Brien to make Connemara doubly important. Against all this barren beauty, the green muffled little spaces of Hertfordshire were, to say the least of it, unexciting. But inside the charmed gates of that Elizabethan gentleman's house, it was, of course, different. There was a long shady drive of noble beeches. There was a knot-garden. There were old lichen-covered classical statues, including a particularly beautiful Diana with face averted towards the woods. There were cherubs doing rude things in the basin of the fountain, and in the centre, disentangling himself from the sculptural seaweed, there was Poseidon.

Inside the house a minstrels' gallery encircled the Great Hall, and on the evening I arrived, when I stepped out of my room, I saw the source of the music which had been drifting up to me as I unpacked. It was a great golden concert harp, and seated at it was a short, composed young woman, with bobbed reddish blonde hair and the blue eyes of so many Florentine paintings. She was not conventionally beautiful, but seated at her harp and playing it like an angel, she could have been taken to be as beautiful as the dusky setting. To me the place had an air of complete unreality. That it should be a school was astonishing, that is until the girls arrived the next day.

Early that morning the headmistress held a staff meeting and told us newcomers about the school. We were privileged to have an international mix of girls who had matriculated in their own country and whose parents wanted to give them this year of exposure to spoken English and English culture generally. *What*, I wondered, *am I doing here?* We would find them quick and responsive for the most part, but should there ever be any difficulties, we should come to her about them and never decide ourselves on punishment. The picture built up at this stage was of a whole schoolful of spoiled brats, each with a personal maid at home, who would be as difficult to deal with as a cageful of monkeys.

They were nothing of the sort. French, Dutch, Iranian, Greek, Italian and Turkish all turned out to be no different from girls anywhere. There was an odd mix of talents and the most remarkable was that of an Iranian girl of nineteen – this was so long ago that she described herself as Persian. She was small, sallow and very dark, with (next to John O'Connor's) the smallest hands I had ever seen stretching without effort over an octave. She spent a lot of time at the piano and I noticed on my way through the Great Hall that there would always be a group of girls gathered around her, listening intently. I didn't at first recognise any of the music, but it was classical in feeling and, within its parameters, quite varied. Frequently they would be quietly giggling and pointing to one another – fairly odd behaviour when most of their fellows were out on the tennis courts.

One day they called me over and Bimala smiled 'For you I have made this', she said, striking up a little dance tune and then embellishing it. So she had heard and loved Elgar's 'Enigma Variations' and decided she could do that too, and had composed a thumbnail sketch for each of her friends? Wrong, because she could neither read nor write music and had never had a music lesson in her life. (Her parents wanted her to study Law). Yet among eight or nine girls she could on request play the little piece composed for each one, and it became a joke that she would play my piece whenever I happened to cross the hall at weekends on my way out for a walk.

Then there was a French girl of seventeen from Rouen called Mathilde. She was a quite ordinary seventeen-year-old in every respect but one: she was an expert dressmaker and designer of clothes and made all her own leisure garments. But she became infantile and hysterical if any of her clothes was accidentally damaged, for instance by having something spilled on it or by catching a skirt or a dress in barbed wire. This happened one day when I was taking a group of girls for a walk to the nearby village. Mathilde snagged her skirt as we were crossing a stile and when she freed the garment there were a couple of little runs in the fine wool – hardly noticeable, in fact. But she set up a loud lamentation like a woman keening a dead child. I had heard of her strange habit but hadn't witnessed it before, so I could hardly believe her shrieks and screams of grief. She refused to proceed to the village with what she called a 'ruined' skirt and I sent her back to the school again accompanied by a friend. Mathilde's screams followed us almost to the village church. The rest of the girls were apparently so used to these excesses that they soon started to talk about something else and when we arrived back to the school again, there was Mathilde sitting cross-legged on the common room window seat with an open workbox beside her and the skirt spread out for restoration with exactly matching wool.

Miss Brodie was an oddity too, but much more fun. Miss Brodie was so described in gold engraving on each of her suitcases – this by the way was long before the movie and long before the title 'Ms' had arrived on the scene. She was Scottish but came from India where both her parents were doctors. She travelled alone in the care of British Airways. She was five years old. Her hair was ash-blonde and held back by an Alice band, and her eyes were small and intensely blue. She was leggy and tall for her age and had a commanding ring to her voice. She liked to be called Miss Brodie rather than Amanda. The school was amused and indulged her.

It so happens that at this school I was introduced to the abomination of kippers for breakfast and I was pleased to see that not even the English girls could make a very tidy job of eating their breakfast because of the bones. It was quite usual for the maids to carry away large portions of fish as well as bones, but not from Miss Brodie's plate. I watched in fascination the first morning I saw her tackling a kipper. Her hands were small and nimble and she was the first at table to finish eating. She put down her knife and fork neatly in the correct position beside the herring's absolutely bare backbone. There was not a morsel left to eat and Miss Brodie looked around with interest at the laborious work her companions had made of finishing their breakfast. She sat with a small composed smile on her face, and waited patiently for the toast to be brought in. I never saw her being less than scrupulously polite to everybody and she was quite kind to those in any sort of trouble, such as the absence of an expected letter when the post was being distributed. I heard Miss Brodie pointing out on one occasion to a weeping girl twice her age that these days the post was not quite what it used to be when postmen (as her Papa often said) were paid less and did more work. The big canvas bag had probably been too heavy and some letters had been taken out to wait until the next morning, said Miss Brodie with disapproval.

One morning the postman brought a very interesting-looking letter for me. It turned out to be from John Green, a literary agent of Hughes-Massie in London and he wanted to meet me the next time I was in town. He said M. J. McManus had recommended me and given him my new address; it was my habit to keep M. J. informed of any change. I reread John Greene's letter, in which he said he would like to talk to me about finding the right publisher for my novel, and maybe I could meet him at the Café Royal the next time I was in London. I was considerably impressed by his being an habitué of the Café Royal. During a free class that morning, I strolled out into warm April sunshine under the baby beech leaves and thought about the resonant meeting-place. Shades of the Bloomsbury Set and, better still, of Wilde, Beardsley, Max Beerbohm and Bernard Shaw. A man whose habitat was so romantic had to be a good thing, and meeting him would certainly be worthwhile.

Now that the novel was finished, a certain reluctance to take positive action about letting it out into the big cold world had taken possession of me. But now, so to speak, the world in the shape of a London agent had come to me for it. I phoned John Green and we arranged to meet the following week. Once again, I wished I owned a briefcase, but when I did own one, I promised myself that it wouldn't be made of that revolting substance called Rexene, or worse still, that new stuff called plastic. It would be the finest hide for me, or nothing.

In the intervening week I checked over my MS once again, and bought in St Alban's at the weekend a good strong cardboard file which I put into an enormous brown paper envelope. I had taken the MS with me on the bus, not being satisfied merely to make measurements! At the time, St Alban's was, and probably still is, an enchanting little cobblestoned cathedral town, with several stationery shops of the sort Jane Austen might have frequented. The cathedral is so majestic that going there could never be resisted whenever business or pleasure took me to the town. On that April afternoon there was an unlooked-for treat. I had an hour to spend before meeting a friend for supper and I decided to start a walk by dropping in to the cathedral.

Its vastness took me by surprise every time. It was almost like stepping through a gate into a separate universe where the only elements were light and sound. The great oaken door sighed to a close behind me and it was as if all the ordinary sounds of a little market town had been silenced from that instant. Great banners of light criss-crossed one another behind the high altar, which seemed half a mile away. St Alban's is a more austere place than Rheims or Chartres or even Fraumunster. It appeals to the brain rather than to the senses.

Wandering again the familiar aisles of this great cathedral, still functioning after almost one thousand years of worship, seemed to me yet another good omen. There was a great book printed here in 1486 (The Boke of St Alban's) just inside the cathedral gates in fact, and furthermore it was also the home of Francis Bacon, who became Viscount of St Alban's. To this same place he returned after all his vicissitudes, and in this same place he did a final revision of his *Boke of Essays* which was then reissued by a local printing press.

William Cowper had been salvaged here after another of his horrendous bouts of depression, salvaged that is by a local doctor called Nathaniel Cotton. Dickens had a connection with St Alban's also. During one of his lecture tours, he stayed at St George's Hotel, just a short stroll down the road.

All in all, the cathedral wasn't a bad place to lay down a heavy parcel containing one's first novel. As I wandered off into the daffodil sunshine of the broad nave, I kept looking back at the brown paper parcel which was the sole occupant of its pew, to make sure that nobody had made off with it. By this time a few other stragglers had come in for Evensong and the great organ was welling up and filling the building. When the high pure voices of the choirboys joined in from somewhere unseen, I found it difficult to drag myself away.

In fact, by the time I actually did emerge into the year 1950 again, the spring light was thickening in Chequer Street and people were hurrying home from work along the cobblestones.

I was already late for my early supper appointment with a friend, so I hurried too until I turned into the lounge of the St George.

A week later I walked more slowly into a more famous lounge in London, that of the Café Royal. I had never before been inside its hallowed doors, but I knew it *had* to have a liveried doorman and that it had to be red and gold and laden with atmosphere inside. It was, and at three-thirty that afternoon, not too crowded. It has always seemed strange to me that one of two people, meeting for the first time, will often correctly identify the right face. On this occasion it was John Green who at once stepped forward from under an ornate gilt mirror to greet me with an outstretched hand. He was a big brown-eyed man in tweeds who exuded the atmosphere of small country inns and local hunt meetings. He seemed much older than my own father and very friendly. I said something gauche and silly about the magic of being asked to meet somebody in the famous Café Royal, that I seemed to have been reading about all my life, and he looked very like my father when asked for an increase in pocket money – usually by one of the boys, not me.

'Of course it's quite a convenient meeting place', he said briskly, 'but nobody drinks here any more.' He lowered his voice, 'There's a much better place just around the corner and you don't have to consult your bank manager about an overdraft before eating or drinking there. Let's go around there now because I want to hear all about your plans.'

Smiling again, with a hand on my elbow, he guided me through the doors which the uniformed flunkey had opened for me only a few minutes earlier. Clutching my heavy parcel under the other arm, I passed through, shocked by what seemed to me such a poor beginning. If I jump ahead from that moment to ten years into the future, I see something of the way I felt on the faces of Benedict Kiely and Mervyn Wall when we met ahead of our appointment with that same John Green in the Standard Hotel in Harcourt Street, Dublin.

'I *hope*', said Mervyn uneasily, 'that we are just *meeting* him here.'

'Why?' said I.

'Because *this*', said Ben sadly, 'is a *temperance* hotel.'

John Green arrived from Kerry very late and he had indeed ordered dinner for four in this same hotel. The gentlemen persuaded him to cancel it, and instead they took us all up to The Green Tureen. It is long demolished now, like the Standard Hotel itself, to make way for a particularly vile office block, but at the time, visitors who knew their Dublin were said to stay at the Shelbourne and dine at the Russell or The Green Tureen, depending on the lateness of the hour. The Tureen was particularly beloved of journalists working late because Cecil Frew never fobbed them off with a sandwich instead of a proper dinner.

But let me get back to John Green in London on the day he became my agent. My memory of him is quite warm despite the initial disappointment. I have no memory whatever of that place around the corner which he implied was preferred by the cognoscenti to the Café Royal, but I do remember how kindly he discussed the possibility of placing my novel with one of the better London publishers; he had learned to trust the judgement of M. J. McManus, he said, and he very much looked forward to reading and handling the novel. He went on to discuss terms and I was too excited to listen. The moment when that parcel, which had occupied a pew for itself in St Alban's, turned into a manuscript in the imposing heavy leather briefcase of a good London literary agent was overwhelming, and I was glad he had another appointment (also in the Café Royal of course!) so that I could savour the event in my own way around the sunny streets of London. On our parting at Piccadilly Circus, John Green promised he would contact me as soon as he had read my manuscript, and he would list for me the likely good publishers who would be interested. Then he shook hands and was lost among the crowds. I was delighted to be alone.

London I hardly knew at the time, and it was a great place for wandering. I derived high entertainment from strolling along Shaftesbury Avenue and identifying the famous theatres whose names I knew from reading Harold Hobson in the *Sunday Times*. In only a few minutes I had seen the St James's Theatre, the Embassy, the Haymarket and the Globe. On that sunny afternoon the foyer doors were open and I noticed the almost universal red carpets and Victorian pier glasses of the interiors, and guess at the excitement a few hours would bring to those same foyers. *St Joan* was running at the New Theatre, and *Ring Around the Moon* at the Globe. I had seen that Christopher Fry translation of the Anouilh play in Dublin and wondered how it would be interpreted here.

It was a year or two later before I was to live in London. I chose my tiny flat in Bayswater for the precise reason that you could easily walk from it to the West End and home again, thereby saving the cost of the Underground. But that afternoon, theatregoing in London was a fairly remote dream because I hadn't discovered the existence of those big transport lorries that wheeled out of London every night. Some more knowing colleague, with whom I spent an evening in London soon after this, showed me how you could pick up a hitch to our village after only a minimum involvement with the driver. The last bus would long since have gone by the time you were ready to leave London after the theatre, and these lorry drivers were at once casually friendly and impersonal.

When you reached your village, you simply asked your driver to stop and you left the exact bus fare on the dashboard in front of him. 'Thanks, luv', the driver would say, and wait until you had scrambled down from the great height of the cabin. Then he'd give a wave and a parting toot of the horn and that would be that. I never heard of any unwanted sexual advances from such drivers. They were doing a service to the public (forbidden of course by their haulage company) and they accepted the little bonus of the going rate for it. That was all.

On the evening of that momentous visit to London, I caught the last bus, however, and strolled in a sort of dream up along the avenue of tall beech trees to the old house. There was not much left of the daylight but because of the small, freshly-sprung leaves, the evening light was green and flickering. It was quiet except for the tiny sounds of nesting birds, doing their last bits of construction work before settling down for the night.

But before I was halfway along the avenue the evening filled up with that mythical song I had known only from John Keats, but up to this had never experienced. It was pure magic, my first nightingale. Even Keats hadn't done it justice. It filled the air and it filled the senses. When it stopped, it was only for a few seconds, and then it started pealing out again, throaty and exuberant and extraordinarily sensual. It sang for itself and it sang to attract a mate. It sang for summer and it sang for joy. Maybe it just sang to establish a territorial right to this enchanted wood, but what matter? It started off again so many times that I wondered were there several nightingales singing their hearts out to one another. I shall never know.

I do know that although I heard the nightingale many times afterwards in that same beechwood, I never again heard it so many times as on that one April night. When the last song died away, I walked slowly up along the drive until the house came in sight, shadowy and tall with its Tudor chimneys. Six or seven of its many windows were lamplit, the curtains still not drawn and the windows open to the spring night. As often before, I noticed that it looked more like a country house than a school. A coach might come rolling up from the other entrance at any moment. But no, it was a school all right.

From one of those open windows came the horrid shrieks of Mathilde, uncontrolled as an infant's cry. Had somebody stolen a sock of hers? Splashed tea on her newest hand-sewn shirt? No, this was serious. She came shouting down one of the beautiful staircases in search of any figure of authority (me?) to report that a blouse she was embroidering for her mother's birthday had been stolen, probably, she added, by her compatriot Claudine. I sighed and told her firmly it would have to wait until the morning, and would she please stop waking up the house and go to bed. As usual when challenged, she stopped at once and went back to her room. I went around checking the locks on the side doors before going to bed myself; I was always last in when I had been up in London. Maybe I hadn't had a drink in the Café Royal, but life was a lot more interesting than it used to be when I was at home working for the government in the cause of widows and orphans.

7

Conducting One's Education in Public

I spent only one year among the nightingale woods of Hertfordshire. The prospect of living in Florence became a fleeting possibility when I was invited to join a party of friends in Italy for July and August. One of them was looking forward to a holiday with her father who lived, she said, only a stone's throw away from the David of Michelangelo, which at that time stood in the narrow street facing the Academy. The money for this trip came from John Green who had got an advance of £100, standard then, when he had sold my novel to Chatto & Windus.

There were many sensible things I could have done with that money, including the payment in advance to London University of my remaining Arts course fees, but I have never regretted furthering my education in my own way, seeing for myself the meaning of the Renaissance in Italy. At school, I had stuck blurry black and white postcards of the David and the Moses and the Botticelli Venus into my history notebook, and, seeing them in the flesh, so to speak, was an overwhelming experience. Getting to Italy by myself (because the others had gone on ahead and I wanted to do some more editing of my novel before joining them) was the most terrifying thing I had ever done. I travelled to Boulogne on the ferry, by train to the Gare du Nord, and splashed out on a taxi from there to the Gare de Lyon. Travelling south from Paris, I sat on one of those ancient wooden-slatted benches of the era, the hardest seat I had encountered since Miss Batty's in primary school. My only hand- luggage was a rucksack, mainly full of books, which at night became a hard pillow.

I had also brought an ancient wooden trunkful of possessions with me from London, the one my grandmother had sailed home with from New York, and I parted from it with great reluctance at Le Havre. The nice ticket inspector told me it would arrive in Italy before me and that I mustn't worry, 'Soyez tranquille, Mademoiselle', he had said in parting, a sweet smile on his well-worn face. So I forgot about my trunk for the rest of the journey.

I remember it was very cold before we headed straight south from Paris and then the heat became pretty horrible. Everybody else in the carriage seemed to have travelled with a bottle of water and I saw why when I jumped out to buy liquid of any kind during what I hoped would be a long stop. There was a mob of other foolish passengers ganging up on the little drinking fountain, all carrying empty glass bottles. When my turn came, I bent my face under the stream of beautiful cold water and opened my mouth at the same time as the whistle shrieked out its departure signal, whereupon I received a smart rap on the head with an empty bottle from the next person in line. Still dripping, but with my thirst hardly slaked, I hurtled myself again towards the train, finding it difficult to recognise my own carriage until the flash of a red-checked shirt seemed to suggest some familiarity. I opted correctly for that open door and as the train began to move, with me poised somewhere in flight between platform and the high step, an arm reached out and dragged me aboard before slamming the door. While I was thanking the man, he offered me a swallow from his bottle but I shook my dripping head and thanked him again. That same fellow before the journey was much older offered me sausage, bread, a bite of goat's cheese and a swig of wine. I offered him one of my two apples and a bar of plain chocolate, which he accepted at the same time as presenting me with his bottle of water, saying he had another in his rucksack.

I think that generous fellow was the reason why I lived long enough to see the dawn breaking in brilliant splinters of light over the Alps at the Swiss frontier. During a brief stop I refilled my bottle of water and noticed how much better the water tasted than the French stuff. The air was pure and fresh and cold. I learned in another epoch of my life that almost everything which makes life pleasanter works better in Switzerland. Showers, in hotels and in private houses, did not scald or freeze you at random but did exactly what you expected them to do when you pressed 'hot' or 'cold.' Lavatories filled up in seconds after flushing and, while we are down at this level, it's only fair to hand it to the Swiss and say that the sewage plants to be seen all over Lake Zurich are a fantasy of camouflage. They look like the sort of walk-in dolls' castles that the children of the rich play in, and, without being told, one would guess that the water of Lake Zurich is clean enough to drink.

On the other hand, even ten years ago, or not much more, it amused some Swiss friends of mine not to reject electric blankets, despite the glittering cold of winter. Instead, they saved up cherry stones in summer and, as their grandmothers had done before them and made little bags of cambric or wool and sewed up hundreds of cherry stones inside. They left the bags all day on the top ledge of their ancient ceramic wood-burning stoves, around whose lower ledges children loved to sit in winter with books or games. The cherrystone bags were lifted down at night and brought up to bed like commercial hot-water bottles. Menstruating girls were particularly fond of them. This was a tradition stretching back for centuries in country places.

I am still travelling third class on my way to Alassio where Italian friends have invited me to dawdle for a couple of weeks by the sea before going on to Florence, and where the friendly French ticket inspector told me my big old trunk would be awaiting me. Only occasionally during that long journey, changing trains at Ventimiglia, did I have the slightest qualms about that trunk. It contained everything I owned, except the clothes I stood up in, and a pair of cotton shorts and some underwear I had thrown into my rucksack with the books in the forlorn hope that I might have got to change on the journey.

The only thing I owned which did *not* travel with me was *La tete de Marie Julie*. It was intended to be immortalised in bronze and aimed at winning some European art competition, which unfortunately it did not. I had been appalled to find the sculptor about to smash it against a wall in Hertfordshire – and had pleaded mercy for it, pretty thing that it was. Its maker had said, 'Take it. Take it now! If I see it still here in ten seconds, I shall smash it.' A Turkish member of staff offered to mind it for me until I returned but, in fact, I never saw it again, despite many phone calls. Apart from that, all my books and notebooks, my plot book and family photographs and most of my clothes were in my grandmother's trunk which did *not* arrive in Italy before me.

'Domani', the railway clerk told me in that hot little station within sight of the Mediterranean. 'Domani, Signorina.' But my trunk did not arrive on the next day, or on the day after. Or even the next. Every morning for the next week I presented myself at the little railway station. The joyful shrieks of my friends came up from the beach. The station clerk was at first sympathetic, and always said the same thing, accompanied by the same smile, 'Domani, Signorina. Domani.' After a week, he began to regard me as an annoyance. He would shrug and roll his eyes at the same time, 'Niente, niente, Signorina.' He had telephoned ten times and sent two telegrams to Ventimiglia and Savona, for which I paid. Neither could report any trace of the missing trunk. The word *baule* is the Italian word I know best to this day. During phone conversations it recurred again and again: 'La baule de la Signorina Irlandese. Si, baule vecchia.'

At first my friends were sympathetic. They helped to compose telegrams. They offered the loan of clothes for evening invitations which, because some of the group had spent childhood holidays in Alassio, were numerous. Most of the clothes on offer didn't fit. Good friends referred to me as slim in those days, while indifferent ones used the word 'skinny'. At any rate I lacked the generous proportions of my female friends and I preferred to live in the navy blue cotton shorts which had travelled with me in my rucksack. I preferred even to swim in them, and wash everything I had worn that day before I went to bed. They would always be dry in the morning.

'Pouquoi elle porte toujours ces petites shortes?' enquired the friend of a friend who had cycled across the Alps from France to join us. Her enquiry as to why I always wore those same shorts was querulous and baffled. Her English was poor and she had only a few words of Italian, so she hadn't really understood the story of the lost trunk. I was beginning to wonder if I had invented it myself when the booking clerk made a suggestion. Perhaps I would like to travel to Savona and see all the unclaimed luggage they had up there? He had once worked in Savona and seen for himself the amount of luggage travellers seemed willing to abandon. It was the first positive suggestion anybody had made, so I bought a return ticket and left behind the little cool breezes and the blue sea and the silky sand to sit once more on hot wooden slats and spend the rest of the breathless morning rattling inland to the city of Savona.

In many ways the misfortune that made this journey necessary was something I was to look back on as lucky. In Ireland, as everybody knows, we knew next to nothing about World War II. In Britain tremendous progress had been made rebuilding the bombed parts. In little Alassio people seemed to live as far apart from war disaster as, for instance, the Achill Islanders had at home. But when I stepped out into the burning heat of noon in the city of Savona, I was stepping into what six years of European war had done to one little corner of Italy. Obviously it must have fared better than Rome, Naples, Turin or Bologna. But I was walking through a nightmare streetscape of collapsed buildings and drifting dust, with heaps of rubble and torn papers everywhere. Sometimes a gaunt chimney-stack stood up against a gable end; nothing else remained of the bank or public building it had once been.

Sometimes I walked – with the aid of a rough sketch made for me by the booking clerk – across cleared acres of red earth and burning heat where a starving dog or a couple of skeletal cats were searching uselessly for something to eat. I was making for a luggage depot which turned out to be partly ruined, like everything else in sight. The few people who shared this desolation with me were poor and seemingly aimless. A man I attempted to get directions from, in words carefully rehearsed, didn't seem to understand a word of my Italian but anyhow he pointed vaguely back in the direction of the railway station from which I had come. Eventually I did make my way back there and found a small fat friendly man with brass buttons on his dusty jacket and a very old regulation cap on his head. He knew a few words of English and, amazingly, seemed to understand my attempts at his own language. He said he would take me to the station master, who kept records of all phone calls and messages about lost luggage. I was eventually ushered in to an upstairs office with another smile and a flourish of the right arm.

'Ecco, Signorina.'

The station master looked depressed and his manner was not at first encouraging. He was very pale, but in a minute or two he made an attempt to smile as he asked me to sit down and vanished into an inner office, returning with a sheaf of papers on a large hook. From among them he proudly showed me my telegrams and several handwritten pages detailing all the phone calls. His depression was gone and he seemed extraordinarily pleased with himself. He looked at my passport and said he thought he could help. He did this by opening the door and shouting, 'Veni, Domenico!' several times. My friendly man in the dusty uniform appeared and the two had a vigorous exchange in such breakneck Italian that I could scarcely catch a word. The station master handed Domenico a long form after having signed it with a flourish, and then he shook hands with me. I thanked him and he said I must follow Domenico who would guide me to the right place. He was actually smiling as we shook hands.

I followed Domenico through the nightmare of rubble again which had once, he told me, been a public square where people used to sit beside beautiful fountains in the evening and girls and boys used to dress up in their best clothes for a stroll through the palm trees. When a starving snarling dog approached us, genial Domenico kicked the poor creature so viciously that it vanished into a hole in the ground. He led me back then exactly the way I had first come until we reached what I had taken to be an empty ruin.

Inside was a flight of steps going down into darkness and silence. It was very cold down there, and a bit spooky. Domenico took my hand in a sweaty paw and squeezed, but this was not comforting, although even today I would resist describing it as sexual harassment. When I wriggled free in the darkness and said 'No!' in my best schoolmarm voice, he didn't try again, but switched on his powerful torch and put his energy into opening the immense door with the largest key I had ever seen. The light switch this time was working and illuminated the warehouse with a dim yellow light that reminded me of a November London fog. In here had been gathered great unsteady-looking heaps of dusty baggage, piled almost to the ceiling. I couldn't imagine where we could start looking for my property among this lot. Domenico shook his head in reassurance and led the way to another gigantic door which had to be opened with a mighty key. Even this was not the last of the anti-theft devices. One more heavily creaking door led into what seemed to be a completely empty chamber, but in the farthest corner was my grandmother's trunk, triple strapped with metal bars and looking no worse than when I had checked it in at the Gare de Lyon all those weeks before. It *was* a large trunk but it looked tiny in the vastness of this room. All that space, those locks, all that elaborate security was simply to guard one little bit of lost luggage. Mine. And, by the way, it transpired that the explanation for its non-arrival was quite simple. There *was* no customs post at Alassio and everybody thought the trunk had been sent to Ventimiglia. In fact, Savona had been judged more suitable, but nobody had lodged this information anywhere accessible.

'Ecco, Signorina. La baule Irlandese!', said Domenico with simple dignity.

I thanked him. I thanked him again. He bowed and then, with unexpected speed, found in the encircling gloom an old trolley built like a battleship. Onto this he hefted my trunk, waving away my offer to help, and then he trundled noisily off. At the end of the third warehouse (or first, depending how you look at it), Domenico called into life a heavy old grime-encrusted lift. It was no time to be finicky. If the historic piece of technology stopped for all eternity when we were half-way up and delivered me into the opportunistic embraces of this good man, so be it. But the ancient technology did its job, and soon we were back again in the railway station with an engine steaming beside us on the platform.

'Ecco, Signorina', said Domenico again, with a dramatic gesture towards (incredibly) the right train, a gesture that recalled for me a childhood circus and the conjuror taking a rabbit from his hat. I followed Domenico to the guard's van into which, with the strength of ten men, he delicately tipped my trunk. Now that it was safe I warmly shook him by the hands to say goodbye. The thought suddenly occurred to me that, after all, nobody was going to check my luggage for contraband.

'Grazie multo, Signor', I said, smiling fervently at him and venturing to offer the equivalent of ten shillings in lire, whatever it was then. It was a huge tip anyway. He quickly pocketed the money, smiled broadly in return and shook hands once more before whipping the station master's form out of his pocket for me to sign.

'Arrivederci, Signorina', he said then and bowed deeply.

'Arrivederci, Domenico', I said. As the train pulled out on cue, I drew a deep breath and sat down happily on the hard metal bands of the trunk. On the way to Alassio I resisted several efforts by the guard to dislodge me into a carriage and at last he shrugged and left me in peace. There was no food to be had during the long hot journey and nothing to drink but I counted that day among the great successes of my life as we drew at last into the familiar sleepy little station whose sea view (subject of countless nostalgic railway posters) was dark blue and quite deserted now with a dozen or so beach umbrellas sweetly furled like sleeping butterflies in the dusk.

I knew the beautiful skyline of Florence in perspective long before I ever entered the city. There were several hills fringed with cypresses, from which it was possible to watch the sun settling into its bed of flames above the Duomo and spreading a melting golden light over the Palazzo Vecchio and the smaller tower of Santa Maria del Fiore. I could identify these not only from the street plan of Florence I had picked up somewhere but from frequent sketches of the main buildings contributed by my Florentine friend and colleague from the school in Hertfordshire. Her mother was an Eastern European who had married into Russian aristocracy, but her birthplace was Florence and it remained an abiding passion of hers.

So from the constant references to the *flower of cities*, I knew many things you don't usually discover in guidebooks. I knew that in late summer you could watch stars falling over the woods of Fiesole, and that sometimes, at the same time of year, people leaned from their balconies to catch fireflies dancing in the dusk – once a well-wined guest of my friend's mother had fallen into the street below but wasn't really harmed.

I knew too what was really quite useful to bear in mind: that the people of Florence, though chic and charming, could be devious and difficult, and despite what you might think, they didn't really like strangers, whom they mostly regarded as inferior to themselves in every way. This came, my friend assured me, mainly from discovering over the centuries that artists who could not make their name in Florence fled to the neighbouring areas and prepared to try again. Those who *did* succeed in Florence were known to everybody in the world – Michelangelo, Donatello, Brunellesci, Veroccio, della Robbia, Botticelli, Cellini – that was only a few of them, Fiametta said. When I wondered were there any writers, apart from Cellini, she said, 'What about Boccaccio? What about Dante?'

As always, I used to go wandering in the daytime by myself, with the aid of a pocket guidebook, and let my feet take me where they would. I would sometimes make an arrangement to meet my friends for dinner and I would sometimes even turn up. A combination of freedom from money problems, however temporary, and sun and intellectual stimulation, as well as the fascination of 'foreignness' made me worse than usual at judging the time of day, and I did not have a reliable watch.

Florence really was, for the moment, the most enchanting city in the world and I genuinely needed to savour it alone if I couldn't have the right company. Florence made my heart beat faster and it reminded me of the person who *was* the right company. He was not only a couple of thousand miles away but no longer – by the tough but right decision of a year before

– any concern of mine. True to form, he was almost certainly the business of somebody else by now, so how silly it was to permit his intrusion. It didn't last long, but he was there in the Uffizi, mocking canvases I loved, there in the lovely museum of San Marco, following me across the courtyard to the calmly beautiful Fra Angelicos. He would have liked their simplicity. The jokes would have died on his curling lips. And he would have approved of the long shadows of Savonarola and stood bemused, as I did, in the little cell of the great Dominican reformer who was destroyed by the forces of obscurantism during the festival month of May 1498, publicly hanged and burnt as a fringe attraction. There was nobody else around that hot morning when I stood in Savonarola's cell but so strong was the desire to share all this that I had to emerge into the sane sunlight and deliberately remember why I had chosen to cut myself off from the most congenial and the most exciting company I had found in my twenty-four years of life.

One night I had decided to get away early (about 2.30 am that is) from one of those unlovely Dublin parties where nearly everyone is behaving badly and most people are drunk. Of course he wanted to stay on and when I went to say goodnight, he suddenly twisted my arms behind my back, crossing them at the wrists and holding them in what felt like a steel trap. 'You'll go when I permit it', he said, in the voice of a stranger. I suppose he was drunk, but I was deeply shocked because I had never encountered such behaviour before. I agreed that I certainly would go when he permitted it, since I wasn't going to take on an unequal struggle. 'But I'll never give you the opportunity to do this again,' I promised. If an apology had followed, even the next day, would I have changed my mind? It is impossible to say after the passing of fifty years, but I don't think so. My strong instinct at the moment of capture was that from such modest beginnings are wife-beaters and abusive lovers made.

So now, more than a year later, I smiled to myself and kicked a little pebble across the peaceful Piazza San Marco, and decided to cut through those narrow crowded streets smelling of poor people and garlic until I came to the river. Across the bridge I would be a stroll away from the Pitti Palace and the Boboli Gardens where I proposed to eat cheese and peaches for lunch, purchased on the way at a street stall. Tonight, I promised myself, I would be on time for a meal with the crowd and until then, there was a whole day to be savoured alone.

I suppose old habits die hard. As an only girl, I spent a lot of my childhood alone and happy. The prospect of jolly company was always more enjoyable than the reality, and I have to admit that the young Italians among whom I found myself were not the easiest of company for a loner like me. There was, for instance, the day when Fiametta invited me to tea at her mother's house. She didn't, she told me, really know her mother very well, but was expected to pay her a visit now and then. The door of the handsome apartment was opened by a maid in a brown and white uniform and we were shown up a shallow flight of marble steps to a door on the first floor. We had to wait in a small reception area inside the door until the mother appeared and led the way into a huge bright salon full of flowers, whose tall windows overlooked the river. She was a short blonde woman wearing a lot of make-up and jewellery and a rather severe smile. She led us to a little table on which were set out cups and saucers and a plate of small round cakes the size of macaroons.

Almost immediately she was called to the phone and the maid, who was about to set down a silver tea pot, was waved away and told to deliver fresh tea later. The lady disappeared into another room and Fiametta, giggling, offered me the plate. 'At least we can eat the honey cakes', she said. They were chewy and delicious, but two were enough for me. Fiametta made shorter work of the whole plateful than Wilde's Algernon made of the cucumber sandwiches, and then she opened a number of drawers in the nearby chest as she chatted about

87

her mother's meanness. No wonder her husband had left her long ago, Fiametta said.

'Was that your father?' I asked her.

'No, my father was the one who followed. He died when I was three. Of starvation, I expect.' She giggled her way through the last of the honey cakes, and then told me she hardly remembered her father. Just his voice, singing 'Amarili' to her at bedtime.

Eventually her mother came back and looked in horror at the empty plate.

'Valentina had a deprived childhood and has never tasted honey cakes before, so I was happy to offer her plenty on your behalf, Mama,' Fiametta said composedly, licking her fingers.

'If you would know how difficult it is to find real honey cakes ever since the war, Valentina, you would control your appetite just a little,' Fiametta's mother said severely, shaking her head at me. She rang the bell for more, and the maid came to verify there were no more honeycakes until the bakery opened in the morning. 'But perhaps some meringues?' No, certainly not meringues. Fiametta went into poorly suppressed explosions of laughter when her mother said she thought she might fancy a water biscuit and some jam instead.

On the way home I asked my treacherous friend why she had lied about the cakes, and this sent her into peals of merry laughter again. The next time I heard such merriment from her was when she arrived at my door early one morning demanding breakfast. I led her to the rather dim and dusty room where my landlady served mine. The room had faded green walls and it seemed to have nothing to do with the glory that was Florence outside. When I had mentioned looking for another place, Fiametta had become defensive and pointed out that the bathroom had a medieval mural of Cupid and Psyche that Ruskin had much admired. So it had, but splashes from the bathwater and clammy hands had long since worn away the sylvan setting *and* both bodies from the neck down, so they could have been anybody. However, Fiametta had known the landlady since she was a child and I was actually grateful to her for teaching me one of my first Italian words. Her teaching style was the direct method. 'Soldi', she said when I went to her that first day. 'Soldi.' When I shook my head, she slid her thumb across the bunched upturned fingers of her right hand. 'Soldi', she kept saying until I paid the rent in advance for my mosquito-ridden little room. I didn't know about the mosquitos until they came visiting that same night.

Anyhow, Fiametta was warmly welcomed by Maria to her breakfast, an excellent bowl of café latté with the usual fresh seeded roll which had apricot jam heaped into the opening. As I sipped my own coffee the pair of them launched into instant hysterically amusing conversation in headlong Italian which was quite beyond my comprehension. When my landlady departed at last to the dark riverine kitchen, Fiametta's eyes were still running with tears of laughter, and she laid her head weakly on my shoulder for support.

'Santa Maria!' she gasped and went on laughing. I disengaged myself and took a mouthful of coffee. '*What* was all that about?' 'I don't know if I should tell you.' She was still choking with laughter. 'But I will. I tell Maria that I am with the Englishman last night – she knows him because he stays with her last year during a week in May. Now he works in Firenze and I am with him last night. Also the night before in his apartment near Signoria. This morning we make love again and again. We have slept only during two hours, you understand. But pronto, after we make love three times he – you have a word for it. Yes. He *faints*. Like dead.' She goes off into peals of laughter again, closes her eyes and clonks her head off the table.

'He faints?' I say. 'But suppose he's had a heart attack? Are you sure he's OK?' 'I do not know,' Fiametta sighs. 'Because I am so hungry. I run away down here for breakfast. He never has any food in his kitchen. Never. Niente.'

'Suppose he's in need of a doctor? Even dead.' This reduces Fiametta to speechless laughter, and immediately afterwards she tucks heartily into her breakfast again. 'Buono,' she murmurs, and I suddenly find I've lost my appetite. This makes her laugh again and grab my roll. 'Don't you think we should walk over and make sure he's OK?' I try again, and once again Fiametta becomes unmanageable with mirth. 'Non sono habituato,' she says. She's not accustomed to someone who takes something so funny so seriously. I give up.

But I grew to love Florence passionately over the following weeks, if not always the Florentines. In fact when an invitation came for four of us to spend a long weekend out in the Tuscan hills at a famously beautiful villa I thought seriously of passing it over in favour of further immersion in the art galleries, particularly the Pitti Palace where I believed a lifetime's browsing would not be too long. It was high up above the city, above the beautiful Boboli Gardens and from its front windows you could look down and see, in tranquil perspective, the towers and domes of that flower of cities. I liked best to look down at it dreamlike in the haze of noonday. It would be around then anyhow by the time I'd walked up from the Arno. The Boboli would be cool and refreshing in the nimbus of sunlit fountains, but as one mounted the grand staircase of the Palace to the Palatine Gallery it would seem actually cold amid all that marble, and very welcoming after the walk.

Some of the Renaissance paintings in this gallery I knew well from reproductions, and best of all I knew the warmth and domesticity of Rafaello's *Madonna detta della Seggiola*, which hung in the parlour of the Mistress of Studies in school. As I may have mentioned, that parlour was a place I got to know very well because daydreaming was a punishable offence in the eyes of some teachers, and the offender was banished from class. The original of that print, which so often watched me from the parlour wall, was carried from the Uffizi up to the Pitti Palace by one of the Medici wives in the seventeenth century – too beautiful to share with the court perhaps?

In many other enchanting Raffaellos up here one was looking through the artist's unglazed windows at precisely that Tuscan landscape of cypresses and little hills which faced the viewer beyond the heat-hazy domes of Florence. Wandering through those unfolding galleries of the Pitti under gorgeous ceilings painted by hands dead now for three hundred years it was possible to lose count of time and only to be aware of the thickening golden light in late afternoon. I hardly remember being hungry – there would always have been a peach or an apple to hand anyhow in my rucksack. Those days there was no food to be had in the art galleries themselves – that would come in the late sixties when the youth of Europe and America were on the move. By then I was anchored with a couple of small children in Dublin and a husband whom I hadn't met in that summer of my wanderings. But he knew of me when he bought the novel which had funded my trip just before he set off himself to cycle from Calais to Rome, through France and Switzerland. It was to be many years before either of us would be footloose again.

Eventually anyhow, something ludicrous happened in Florence which delayed my trip to Tuscany. On the afternoon of my departure I took a cold bath before meeting my friends at the Duomo. It had been a stifling day in early August and we were to pick up a lift at the Duomo. For me locking the bathroom door was a reflex action although nobody was in the apartment at the time. It was a major mistake, as I learned, too late, that people had locked themselves in before. The lock was one of those fine heavy old brass ones, the best part of 200 years old, and it had been giving trouble since some birdbrain had painted it over on the inside. It was easy to lock the door but for some reason exceedingly difficult, if not impossible, to unlock it from the inside. You had to be released by somebody from the outside. And as I've said, the apartment was silent and empty that hot afternoon.

At first I refused to believe that I couldn't, given time, open that lock, but the first hour passed in increasingly clever but unfortunately futile attempts. I bullied and coaxed the lock by turns, pitting against it all my strength and then flicking at it with what was supposed to be a casual movement of the wrist by way of pretence that nothing was wrong. Something was very wrong indeed, and in my heart I knew after that first hour, that I wasn't going to open the door without help. My friends had probably given me up by now and were well on their way to Siena. It was still possible that Maria might be back early from her work, and when she released me I could pick up a lift myself to Siena. On the other hand, Maria lived an unpredictable life, and she might be babysitting or otherwise occupied overnight on the other side of town.

If the friends came back on Monday morning I might be found alive, otherwise there might just be a few lines before the sports news in the *Irish Times* under the caption 'Irish novelist dies in Florence.' I was only just fit to be described as a novelist since the publication of my first book in April and the story would mention the mysterious circumstances surrounding my untimely death, the locked door, the friends helping the police with their enquiries. 'Whom the Gods love' would be the touching inscription on my tombstone and I'd have a lovely funeral. Maybe even those critics who hadn't liked the book would be forced to eat their words and mention 'youthful promise'.

These deranged thoughts were the result of hunger, so I decided to force open the window at the end of the bath. It probably hadn't been opened for about fifty years, ventilation being provided by a small opening at the top. I made an assault with the bath brush on the latch within reach, but the surprise was on me. A loud crack preceded the disappearance of the entire pane of glass, which I could hear shattering itself in some courtyard far below. My horror was soothed by a breath of sweet cool air as I leaned from the bath to look out. No escape. Sheer stone between me and the next window either side. No ledge of any sort. We were three storeys up above the Arno – and incredibly nobody living around seemed to have heard the noise.

A smoky rose sky received the last strength of the sun and from the apartments all around came the sound of the evening meal being prepared, the clatter of heavy frying pans and the tinkle of china, babbling voices, and with them the delicious whiff of garlic. Italians make an extraordinary variety of noises doing the simplest things and my calls for help went unheard, amid the shouts and squeals and laughs of ordinary conversation. It was half past eight by now and I was starving, so I gave up, climbed over the steep edge of the bath and tried again and again to force the lock of the door. No use. I spoke aloud all I could remember of Yeats 1919 (*Many ingenious lovely things are gone/That seemed mere miracle to the multitude*). I closed my eyes in concentration trying to remember what happened after that. When I opened them again the rosy lights had died and dusk fine as ashes had started to drift down into the courtyard. The light switch was outside the bathroom door, so even if I'd had a book to hand I couldn't have read it.

I tried calling again from the bath and this time a hugely fat young man from an open window far below began to mime a proposition which didn't seem to me like a good idea even if it were feasible, so I stepped out of the bath again and began contemplating the distressed murals. In the distance, someone began to sing *La Vie en Rose* (the great song of that year) in a sickly sweet tenor and later on out of the darkness came the vicious squabbling of, possibly, a husband and wife. Was it a weekly routine this screaming match? This was Friday and the faded light told me it was now ten o'clock, four hours after I had locked myself in. I was now so hungry that I was in danger of eating the soap. No doubt the friends had long since given me up and were sitting replete under the vines on some country balcony, surrounded by delicious leftovers – risotto or cannelloni or that Florentine delicacy of grilled lambs' brains.

Two hours, another despairing bath (it would be nice to be found a clean corpse at least) and many Yeats poems later, plus half of *The Lady of Shallot*, I heard the joyous sound of the flat door opening. I began to beat on the glass panels in front of me with both hands. I could hear Maria running along the stone passage and calling to me at the same time to be careful of her valuable bathroom door. When she released me I realised that, although six hours may not be long term imprisonment, it was long enough to convince me that I must continue to live a very law abiding life to avoid a jail sentence. The furore created by Maria over her crashed window pane also told me it was time to start moving on. But it would have been time anyhow, as the next few days proved.

There is a moment in every year, and I've always been conscious of this wherever in the world I happen to be, when lengthening shadows or the movement of birds or a single chilly breeze at the end of a long hot day or the merest whisper of dryness in the tent of leaves above one's head or the thinning of the crowds in a tourist street – any of these signs – set off a small alarm in one's head. Time to move on. Time to remember that summer is so precious simply because it is so transient, and the suspension of work, so blissful at the start becomes a worry as the days imperceptibly grow shorter. But I didn't leave Italy all the same until the money (that magical sum of one hundred pounds) had dwindled to what *might* provide enough travel money back to England in addition to my return ticket. No likely job had materialised to justify selling it at a bargain to a homing friend who had had what I lacked, the confidence to buy only a single ticket. But before I left for England, I did spend a few days rambling in Siena. I arrived in just immediately after the madness of the Palio, with its fallen banners, its littered ribbons and favours, its exhausted air of going back to sleep again until next year. This of course was nonsense, but the feeling was accentuated by the fact that I walked into Siena during siesta time, when there was virtually nobody about and when every sleeping dog gave you to understand that he wouldn't even move an eyelash until the afternoon shade had stretched across his alley.

Even denuded of its people, dozing behind their closed green shutters, Siena interested me quite a bit because of its maverick Saint Catherine whose life had been slightly modified for us in school. She lived in the fourteenth century but she was no white robed milksop. She defied her father in the matter of matrimony and joined the Dominicans at the age of sixteen. Instead of sinking comfortably, after some years, into her reputation as a mystic who spent most of her days caring for the sick poor, she wrote a brisk and critical letter to Pope Gregory IX urging him, in effect, to rise up out of the fleshpots of Avignon and return to his proper duty as the Bishop of Rome and the governing of his church in the place of its foundation.

The exile in Avignon had been going on for about seventy yeas at the time, and it's probable that successive Popes had begun to prefer the freedom, the luxury, perhaps the beauty of the little French town, to the stresses and splendours of Rome. When, not surprisingly, Gregory did not return to Rome as requested by an obscure provincial nun, she packed her bags and set off on horseback to persuade him. This was in 1376 when she was in her late twenties and that journey, amazingly, resulted, the following year, in ending what had become known, under the influence of the French Popes, as the Babylonian Captivity. It was impossible, as I stood alone in the cool little church of St Catherine on that sultry afternoon, to imagine the sort of flamboyant courage and sense of destiny that had carried her over the mountains from central Italy all those hundreds of miles away to the heart of southern France. What sort of conviction made the quiet mystic, who fed and washed each day the most depressing and abandoned of the sick poor, leave them to the care of her community while *she* travelled on her self appointed diplomatic mission to see the head of her church? What sort of polemic made her succeed? The answer was not to be found in the little quiet church named after her, nor in the somnolent streets littered with coloured favours after the Palio.

But Tuscany was undoubtedly beautiful. The little hills were clothed with cypresses and olive trees and the stone villages through which I walked, on and on, in the lengthening shadows of a September sun were golden and cool and seemed to hold on to the light. But the dusk came fast all the same, sudden as a snuffed candle and I was miles away from the country house where a bed awaited me. I had a rough sketch map of the place and three matches left in my rucksack but as I've explained before, my sense of direction is deficient, and somewhere I took a wrong bend in the road, and found myself walking along for miles in the dark until the moon came up big and silvery between the cypresses. There was no other light anywhere, no buildings except the odd little country church. Locked, I'm afraid.

However the darkness was cheered by the continuing chatter of the cicadas – I loved the word, and I loved the sound, the bright conversational rhythms of it. Even although the small creatures were all around me, I'd never seen one in my life until next morning. And how had it suddenly become next morning?

The answer is simple. Hot and thirsty, I sat down by the sandy roadside to eat two ripe peaches and take a slug or two of warmish water from my rucksack. Suddenly, despite a persistent waking dream of roasting coffee beans drifting out through Bewley's window in Grafton Street, life didn't seem so bad. I was alone and free in a classically familiar landscape of the Renaissance. I wasn't hungry and I wasn't thirsty any more. I had good walking shoes, no blisters, and a change of socks. There was a moon up and maybe half a million cicadas singing to me for company. In the moonlight a warm breeze from the hills brushed back my hair, and I was beginning to be sleepy. The light was beautiful, but not for reading although I had a well-thumbed Boccaccio in my rucksack. The grass beside the little road was soft and springy and a canvas rucksack wasn't the worst of pillows. I certainly can't remember deciding to go to sleep, but the next thing I was aware of was the dewy dampness of my clothes and the enormous red arc of the sun emerging above the skyline, and then a thin morning chorus of birds while the almost tireless cicadas gave them a chance. Those cicadas would be wakened later by the heat of the sun. But meanwhile this *was* morning.

Despite my stodgy resistance to camping out in the cold wet climate of home, I was awake and delighted with myself after having slept all night in the warm scented darkness of Tuscany. Lifting my head from the rucksack I saw that I had crushed under my cheek a large strange insect, sandy and almost colourless, with a rather flat triangular head and bug eyes, now dimmed for ever. His wings were folded, long, pointed and transparent and I suddenly knew that I had seen my first cicada. Sad that it had to be a dead cicada and that it was I who had almost certainly stilled his summer songs for ever.

It is that morning I remember fifty years after when somebody says 'Italy'. What I have hardly any memory of at all is eventually finding the small country mansion later that day and finding also the friends who had arrived the day before. I know from scribbled notes on the back of my map that I *did* find them and from those same notes that our host, the son of the house, had smashed into four pieces, when he was fourteen, an original della Robbia medallion, because his father had annoyed him by some command or other. He had accurately targeted the treasure with a heavy leather football and its mended pieces had been reattached to the left of the hall door.

The summer wore away, and as my funds diminished and no real job had materialised, it seemed that using my return ticket to London was a necessity. One small job, however, delayed my departure for a week, but there was no money in it. I was offered a free studio apartment not far from the river by the sculptor friend of a friend who had to visit his parents in the country, and needed somebody each day to dampen down some large plaster models he had made which were covered in old bed sheets. The reason why they had to be kept moist I have now forgotten but it meant, for me, prolonging my stay in a city I had grown inordinately fond of over the couple of months I had known it.

All I had to do was water a few plants and keep the sculptures moist, in return for a roomy apartment near Signoria whose only bed was in the studio. Waking up to confront the ghostly, arcane shapes under their shroud could be disconcerting, but the whole deal was amusing, especially the finale. I had to carry, as a last service to the sculptor, a small bronze commissioned by a client in Paris. He would meet me at the Gare de Lyon wearing a red camellia – I must wear a red camellia too, pinned to my left shoulder, and if questioned by anybody in the course of the journey I must say that the sculpture was myself, commissioned by my father. The point behind all this was that, at the time in Italy, and possibly still, it was an indictable offence for any foreigner to take a work of art out of the country – except for commissioned portraits.

The glamour of this assignment took my mind off the melancholy of the long train journey north, away from the sun, away from so many happy wanderings and back to work again on a second novel about which I wasn't very happy. In order to buy time for work anyhow, I had to find some sort of job, most likely teaching again. The first pay cheque would be at least a month away and I had to find a place to live which had a steady table or (impossible aspiration) a desk to offer. But why look so far ahead? There was the last of the lion-coloured

South of France, the *Sud*, rushing past the window, people on the hilly slopes working on the *Vendages*, the grape picking, preparing for the annual drama of wine making. In the fullness of time, I was to have a student daughter who would clock up quite an amount of money for her winter diversions at just that *Vendages*, but at the time I'd never heard of anybody but the local people working their own vines. Italy was already in the past and soon the *Midi* was too, and we were passing through a succession of dull industrial landscapes around Lyon, and ugly little provincial towns like the one which so enraged poor Emma Bovary that she destroyed herself in her efforts to bring excitement into her life. And then at last the outskirts of Paris and the realisation that there was only one more piece of excitement for me – identifying the gentleman with the red camellia and handing over his property before the dash across Paris to catch my connection at the Gare du Nord.

I had to face the fact that I had virtually no money left and that the experience of real hunger was not too far away. Meanwhile how many gentlemen might there not be at the Gare de Lyon wearing a red flower? Was I *really* sure what a camellia looked like from a distance? I didn't have long to worry. I was claimed almost immediately by a plump youngish man in black, wearing little winking gold spectacles like Mr Pickwick's, and the most approving of smiles to match his camellia. He took the wrapped head tenderly out of my arms, as though it were indeed his child, and invited me most warmly to lunch with him. I was of course starving by this time but it was a question of lunch or my connection for the boat.

'Vous etes tres gentille, monsieur, mais il faut que je prends le train a Boulonge presque tout-de-suite.'

'Quelle dommage!' he sighed, and took my considerably reduced baggage in one hand, while keeping a firm grip on the head under his other arm.

'Let me carry this one step further to the taxi,' I said, and he laughed as I took it. A charming laugh, even if he *was* an art smuggler. Outside, amid streaming crowds of people on their way to lunch, he emitted a piercing whistle and held up one arm at the edge of the pavement. Clearly recognising a fellow Frenchman in a hurry, a taxi pulled up smartly at our feet, and the taxi man replied to the hurried request: 'A quelle heure arrive cette loco?'

'A douze heures et demi,' said I, and both men gasped together.

'Zut, allors, allez!' My friend the smuggler handed over what was obviously a generous advance fare, and I threw myself into the back of the taxi after handing over the piece of sculpture for the second time.

'Merci, Monsieur,' I said.

'Merci, merci Mademoiselle!' The tone was fervent, the smile more charming than ever as he put a business card into my pocket, and his torn camellia into my hand. 'Au revoir, Mademoiselle. Et quand vous arriverez encore a Paris, n'oubliez pas!' He indicated the pocket where he had put his card and slammed the taxi door. 'Bon voyage, Mademoiselle.'

I had only ever seen people in movies waving handkerchiefs in farewell, but he waved his large white one as I began the most terrifying taxi drive of my life. This driver was going to earn his large tip even if it meant killing himself (and me!) which he very nearly did. Taxis and cars hooted furiously after us, but the driver was equal to the challenge. He screamed around corners in the best movie style, and I held tightly on to the seat in front and told myself that I *couldn't* be feeling sick, it was just hunger. But we did make it – with only seconds to spare. It must be remembered that this was in the age before the species porter became extinct, and if you were young and in need and female they didn't always expect a tip. I had nothing to give anyhow, except a spare red flower and I held on to that for good luck. Luck I had. I literally threw myself on to the train and the thrice-blessed porter threw my luggage in after me before slamming the door. There was only about £2 left in my rucksack pocket, but I had had a never-to-be-forgotten summer in Italy and I was on the second last lap of the return journey to London. Smugly, I regarded that hundred quid from the publishers as very well spent.

8

The Wand of Harlequin

Back in London I found my bedsitter in Bayswater, which as in Florence had to be paid for in advance. This tidily consumed all my remaining cash. Even during the so-called Emergency, there had always been enough food in our house, and quite often we also had luxury items like oranges or white bread or Nescafé from one of my father's numerous friends. I had never been hungry in my life, except briefly cycling home from school in the afternoons when other girls had pocket money and could go home sucking their Cleeves toffee or Rollos. Pride sometimes made me refuse a share, on the rare occasions when an offer was made. Remember you didn't just need money, you needed sweet coupons as well and honour demanded that you buy the sweets next day. So I would usually cycle on ahead by myself, taking wilful enjoyment from my sin of pride.

But the sort of hunger I experienced for about three days in London was different. I could, of course, have eaten properly if I had put my few pounds (supplemented from a now empty Post Office account) into food instead of into a large bright bedsitter in Bayswater with gold velvet curtains to match its carpet and a beautiful desk looking out over a whitewashed balcony which caught every ray of Autumn sun and had one wall covered in Virginia creeper. I could have dossed down in a hostel, I suppose, but the idea scared me – I'd never shared a room in my life, not even with a sibling, as I've probably said, because I was the only girl in my family. But I had never been hungry either, so the priority of the first few days was to find a job, which meant keeping money for the bus or underground. The strategy was to buy milk, bread and cheese and nothing else except an apple or a banana in the middle of the day. That way one could stay healthy.

But one chilly wet day, too early for the interview I had that afternoon, I took shelter in Lyons Corner House and warmed my hands on a cup of coffee. I was tormented by the smell of scrambled eggs and bacon on toast, of chips and sausages, even of boring old shepherd's pie which everybody at the tables around me seemed to be enjoying. Two women in soufflé hats were discussing which Lyons produced the best shepherd's pie. One of them said West Ken and the other one plumped for one at the top of Oxford Street – she said all her family thought the same because the mashed potato on top was much browner and crispier and they used more meat inside. Hastily finishing up the coffee, I went out into the rain and bought a postcard of the changing of the Guard for my father.

On top I wrote my new address and then this: 'You won't be surprised to hear I have a slight end-of-holiday cash flow problem until my first month's salary comes through – could you loan me a fiver, JJ?'

I stamped and put it in a letter box before I could change my mind, but three days later I hadn't got a reply, so I counted all the people I knew who were probably in London at that moment. There were three: my agent, my publisher and Elizabeth Emmanuel. She was the tall dark-eyed buyer in a bookshop not far from the Embankment. I plumped for Elizabeth, to whom I'd been introduced at a very small lunch party given by my publisher, and later I had often chatted to her while browsing in the shop. However on this occasion it took me ten minutes of holiday chat – she remarked on how tanned I was – and five minutes of book babble before I could come to the point. I was even half-way out of the shop, but I forced myself to go back.

'Oh, by the way, I'm completely cleaned out until my father's cheque comes through – could I possibly borrow a pound, Elizabeth, to be paid back in a day or two?'

'But of course, my dear,' Elizabeth said with her kindest and most beautiful smile. 'Hold on a sec. Oh, by the way, we sold 10 copies of your book since you went abroad and I've just ordered more.' By the time she came back, I had hidden my scarlet face in a history of archaeology by Mortimer Wheeler. Elizabeth was apologetic, peering into her handbag. 'Do you know I have this mean habit of keeping myself deliberately short of cash to avoid overspending and all I have in here just now is nine shillings – '

'O, honestly, it's all right – the post will probably have come by the time I get home. The old man never lets me down.'

'Come back here this minute,' she ordered. 'What I mean is, I've had to give you a cheque – made out to 'cash to bearer' so you won't have any trouble at the Midland around the corner. Here m'dear.'

Still smiling like an angel, she handed me my salvation, but that wasn't the nicest thing I remember about her. A few days later I went in to pay her back and she thanked me with incredible grace: 'You've no idea how nice it is to have some cash without the trouble of making time to go to the bank. Thank you so much, Val, my dear. I feel quite rich, I promise you.'

I left the bookshop almost feeling that I had done *her* a favour, but I have to say she wasn't the only delightful English person I encountered during that three year stint across the pond. Nor indeed, was she the only English-Jewish friend I made. But she was the only one I ever borrowed money from and even to this day, I'm astonished that I could make myself do it. Likewise, I'm even astonished that I could bring myself to the point of borrowing money from my father. Even as a child, I never asked for pocket money. I took it with some surprise, if it was offered. It was several years into the future that I learned from my husband the basis for this reluctance. He called it a 'low threshold of embarrassment', and he had it too. It had a wider application, of course, than mere shyness about borrowing money from somebody, but I won't digress into amateur psychology.

Having some money in my pocket again in addition to a really pleasant place to live, just a minute's walk away from Kensington Gardens and the Albert Hall, was wonderfully cheering. I had a job of sorts too, at a theatrical school for children where the pupils were learning a much harder lesson than anything on the syllabus. They were learning to take success and failure – in the matter of auditions, for instance – with the same bland smile which was their best defence. It astonished me how free from natural envy they seemed to be when an unexpected child succeeded instead of themselves. They were already schooled to hug and congratulate. What they really felt was hard to gauge. Some of them were the children of well-known stage performers who, no doubt, had learned from their cradles how to defend themselves behind a mask of indifference or excitement. Most were not, but were the product of mothers to whom Noel Coward gave that celebrated advice 'Don't put your daughter on the stage Mrs Worthington.' There were at that school about half as many boys as girls and the competition was not so punishing. Looking back, it's the boys I remember better, and later I recognised a few of them in *Oliver*. One of the boys called John Lever had a surprising maturity for an eight year old. I took him aside one day after class and asked him would he promise not to keep on distracting certain classmate who, perhaps, didn't pick up their work as quickly as he did. I pointed out to him how frequently some of those children were absent at auditions and the absolute necessity for them to make use of every uninterrupted session in the classroom.

John spun a pencil between two fingers and looked up seriously into my face. He was a very small boy for his age with a pale face and steady hazel-brown eyes. 'I'll think about what you said, Miss,' he promised, 'and I'll tell you before the end of the week.'

Was he just a *very* good actor already, or was he serious? There wasn't long to wait. He appeared at my desk very early on the Thursday with a short white carnation, whose stem was circled with silver paper, and a leather bookmark he had made himself, wrapped up in silver paper too. 'I've been thinking,' he said. 'I won't mess around and tell jokes in class again. I only do it for fear I'll forget them – do you know the feeling?' I did.

'Thanks, John', I said, accepting both pledges of sincerity for what they were and trying to conceal the fact that I was rather moved by the maturity of this odd child. There was no more trouble in class from John ever again, and I've often wondered what life made of him. If he succeeded as an actor I haven't heard of it, but I'm pretty certain he has succeeded as a thoroughly dependable human being.

Nineteen-fifty-one was a good time to be in London. I didn't know the city well enough to mourn the demolition of many old buildings on the south bank of the Thames as I was to do bitterly a decade later in Dublin. The organisers of the South Bank Exhibition had distributed around the city a number of lushly written pamphlets. This is how one of them began: 'Harlequin, with a resounding whack of his slapstick gave the signal for the Grand Transformation. Gradually the whole scene turned or sank or rose out of sight,' (Pardon?) 'leaving instead a glittering fairy palace, a scene of unbelievable enchantment. And indeed Harlequin's magic bat has perhaps touched the backdrop of London, for how different the great city will be in 1951 from what it was, say ten years ago!'

That copywriter was certainly spot on when he compared the London Season of the Arts 1951 with what I can only imagine was the London of 1941, war-battered, hungry, dark, and almost denuded of its young people through recruitment or evacuation to the country.

Apart from the hot and dusty days that summer, I remember some superb nights of theatre: *Electra* for instance, at the Old Vic, and then *Twelfth Night* and the *Merry Wives of Windsor*. Robert Atkins put on, in Regent's Park, a marvellous open-air production of *A Midsummer Night's Dream*, for which actual avenues of trees and a full moon provided the setting, and the night air seemed as warm as noon. My companion on those occasions was Francis Odle, whose ambition was to write a biography of George Orwell; he had devoured the novels as a young conscript. His reward for this war effort, incidentally, was subsidised entrance to Oxford University, which his family could not have provided. I owe to Francis long sunny days wandering under the dreaming spires. We used to cycle to Oxford now and again at weekends, and because Francis had one or two friends still trying (but not very strenuously) to pass their exams, we could go punting on the river with them. I had read *Brideshead Revisited* and fancied that some of Sebastian Marchmain's Oxford still lingered among the willows. And the antique shadow behind Sebastian was The *Scholar Gypsy*. My own early morning sessions of do it yourself study at home already seemed long ago and very far away.

Francis had a teasing and amusing quality to his friendship. Like my Uncle Pat – the only one of the uncles who had made it into a senior civil service job – he liked to turn up for the theatre in filthy old tennis shoes to make a joke of his otherwise conventional rig-out and he liked to eat chips from a newspaper amid a smartly dressed crowd coming out from the theatres. We both lived within walking distance of the West End, and one night I bought him supper in a place called Milland's in Notting Hill because I had just received a cheque from *The Irish Press* for a poem. He said he would treat me on the way home from Alec Guinness's *Hamlet* which we were going to see later in the week. I hoped he wouldn't choose the same place because there were many other restaurants I hadn't tried.

Francis did not choose the same place for supper. Somewhere in the vicinity of Marble Arch, he disappeared through a doorway and reappeared carrying steaming newspaper parcels of fish and chips, one of which he handed to me before diving into his pocket and presenting me with two large tissues. He refused to consider disposing of his newspaper in the next litter bin on the Bayswater Road, where I naturally stopped. The printers' ink in newspaper was, he said, part of the essential flavour of good fish and chips. He said it seeped gently through the brown paper bag covering the chips, and no gourmet would dream of removing it before the chips had been consumed. No, of *course* it wasn't dangerous to human beings – in fact printers' ink was an essential part of the nutrition, Francis said.

'It would spoil the flavour for me,' I said firmly.

'You just don't *want* to walk along a London street eating out of a newspaper,' he said accurately. 'That's all it is.'

'That is all it is. The ghost of my granny would haunt me if I did.'

'I *challenge* you to do it. Apart from tasting this British delicacy as it should be served, you'll be breaking a self-imposed (or worse granny-imposed) taboo. Go on, Mulkerns. Do it!'

I did it. Francis is dead now, and I'm glad I did what he asked. And very delicious the printers' ink tasted too. Francis skipped along in his unspeakable runners, happy as only those who have recently converted the heathen can be. He had more to offer. He knew by heart long passages of Chaucer's Wyf of Bathe and he had a delightful mother, straight out of *Cider with Rosie*, who sometimes invited us to what she called her place in the country. Biggin Hill was never free of planes zooming overhead or the lighter noises of the constant traffic along the road below her cottage. And he had an equally delightful friend called Richard Baker who, one afternoon, invited us to a guitar session by a young, very promising artist called Julian Bream. Richard was recording him for an autumn radio programme on the BBC. With sun blazing away outside (1951 really was a flawless summer), we sat and listened to the cool Spanish night this young boy was creating for us with his music. When he had finished and become again a shy schoolboy unsure of himself in alien surroundings, neither Francis nor I could believe it.

However, the artistic delights of that summer were not over yet. We took a steamboat at Embankment, where Harlequin had already made his transformation of banners and lights, and we went upriver to Hampton Court Palace for a concert of madrigals. On Francis' suggestion, we stayed outside in the gardens after the interval to hear how this typical Tudor music by Orlando Gibbons sounded among the trees. We listened as it drifted and became one with the sounds of the river. That music was formal and melancholy and extraordinarily beautiful:

> I saw my lady weep
> And Sorrow proud to be advanced so
> In whose fair eyes where all perfections keep.
> Her face was full of woe
> But such a woe (believe me) as wins more hearts
> Than mirth can do with her enticing parts.

Francis said he had grown passionate about madrigals at Oxford, when had joined one of the music societies, and it was he who told me that one of the greatest composers of this type of music was an Irishman at the court of Queen Elizabeth I, one John Dowland. And, by the way, during that summer in London I became aware that among some, being Irish had a sort of cachet. People tended to come up to you at gatherings and tell you that their grandfather or maybe great-grandfather was Irish. Other types, usually women, would remark that their mothers had always preferred Irish servants because you can train them successfully from scratch; they never came burdened with any theories or preconceived ideas about service or hygiene.

One evening at a party in Paddington (it must have been one of the last privately owned houses in the district), a hard-pressed hostess thought she had found a solution to too many guests arriving at the same time by introducing me to a group more or less unknown to one another and also to me. 'She's an Irish writer. She'll have you in hysterics with the story of how they lost her trunk in Italy.'

The woman vanished and I looked uneasily around at the circle of bored or slightly hostile faces and suddenly I knew the meaning of the actor's tag 'I died that night.' I failed rather miserably as an entertainer because, in that setting, the story no longer seemed funny to *me*, even the bit about the old inspector in Savona who came along pleased as Punch because he had found, neatly tagged, a record of every telegram which had been sent to him from Alassio. That was one of the occasions when I asked myself: What am I *doing* here?

Suddenly I caught sight of the alert cheerful face and the high prematurely bald dome of Francis Odle above the other heads crowding through the door, and everything changed. He spotted me at once and came beaming over to the rescue in his flapping canvas shoes. In no time at all he had a party going before we moved happily away from that formerly dead corner of the room.

The evening was salvaged Francis' arrival, but the question remained: what, in fact, *was* I doing there? I had been in England three years, I had finished and published one novel, and begun another, but I spent most of my days teaching in a dead end job because I lacked the *real* interest to spend more time studying for a proper qualification. It was clear that I *could*

110

teach, but it wasn't enough for me. And, besides, I came to that activity which I regarded as my proper job late in the evening and quite tired after a day in school, enjoyable though it nearly always was. Eventually I decided to give it one more school year – I had committed myself to a year anyhow – and then see what Dublin had to offer.

There was *The Bell* still clanging away over there, although Seán Ó Faoláin had tired of the grind and had yielded his place as editor to Peadar O'Donnell. Peadar I knew slightly and I greatly admired his novel *Islanders* which he always said he wrote only to pass the time in jail. However, even on his release he wrote other books so that didn't wash. There might be some hope from the quarter of M.J. McManus (who continued to be kind and ever helpful to me) and who was still literary editor of *The Irish Press*, but by then I knew a little about the hierarchy in newspapers. Literary editors seldom had the power to hire or fire, and what I wanted at that stage was just enough money to live on independently in Dublin while I got on with writing novels. In other words, I wanted the moon, and surprisingly I got it.

9

And Did You Not See Shelley Plain?

Towards the end of the school year I went over to Dublin to see my father, and one hot, humid day at the end of June I suddenly remembered the exact location of the *Bell* office as I stood on O'Connell Bridge to catch a breeze coming up river from the docks. The Liffey at low tide was sluggish, and smelled no sweeter than usual, but the breeze was invigorating and after a few breaths of it I decided to take a chance on finding Peadar in the office.

I well remembered that stuffy little place at the top of the narrow staircase of 14 Upper O'Connell Street. I remembered my introduction to 'close editing' by Harry Craig, when he reduced an early story of mine to half its length and greatly improved it, though I certainly did not think so at the time.

When I knocked, Peadar said 'Come in' with an abstracted air, and when I did he was standing still scratching his grey head in the middle of the chaotic office and, as though four hours instead of four years had elapsed since we had last met, he said, 'Take a perch, child, and tell me what to do with all this.'

'All this' was the tumbled papers, the dusty galleys hung layer over layer on the walls, and even hanging down from

112

the heaps of back numbers on the window ledge. There was a general air of *laissez-faire* which, from the direction of Peadar's hopeless gesture, seemed to be concentrated on several heaps of (probably) unsolicited manuscripts from ever-hopefuls like myself not so long befoere. I gingerly edged away a pile of letterheads on the smaller of two tables to make a place for myself, presumably the perch to which he had referred. Peadar paced the very small square of floor and ran his fingers across the white tufted eyebrows.

'What I'm in need of is a bit of help', he said. 'The help I had has taken itself off to London.'

'Coincidentally, Peadar, what I need is a job. I'm thinking of coming home again from London, as it happens.'

'Are you now?' said Peadar, raking me suddenly with his extraordinarily youthful-looking bright blue eyes. 'Frank O'Connor said you wrote a good book.' Question and statement were fused in the guttural Donegal growl. He suddenly looked crafty. 'How much could you live on in Dublin?'

'By that I take it you mean how little?'

'You're quick on the uptake, I'll say that for you,' Peadar grinned suddenly, showing some of the tumbled hound's teeth, very white still because he never smoked. 'What's more important is, can you start at once? We can discuss minor matters later on. Come over to Bewley's for a coffee.'

'Thanks, I will. If we do come to an agreement, I could probably start the week after next.'

'If the bailiffs haven't got here by then.'

Very generous in some ways, but country-cute in others was Peadar. Instead of asking how much I could live on, an offer to match the salary of the last associate editor might have been more fair, but then this was a decade before Women's Lib, and it was generally accepted that women cost less to hire than men. In fact, when it came, Peadar's offer suited me very well. I told him that one of the reasons I wanted to leave London was that, by the time I got home from work by Underground in the evening, I was pretty tired and disinclined to work hard enough on my new novel. If I could work at home on it in the mornings, when I came back to Dublin, and be in to the *Bell* office not later than two o'clock every afternoon, I would stay on and work for as long as it took, especially coming up to publication day. If I could do that I would be entirely satisfied to accept his offer. It would (together with fees for reviewing, broadcasts and freelancing in general) give me enough to live on independently in a flat within walking or cycling distance of O'Connell Street. So it was settled, over a second cup of coffee. I couldn't believe my luck.

Peadar was, in most ways, a maverick, but in one way he was a completely conventional writer. He hated actually sitting down to write. Even before I went to work for him, I suspected this because of the brevity of, or quite often the absence of, his editorials on that notably editorial magazine. Ó'Faoláin had sometimes been in danger of filling a whole issue with what he wanted to say, and to this day, those editorials make marvellous reading. Peadar's were brief, staccato, sometimes baffling in syntax, and greatly in need of the actual physical presence that would have given them impact, say, at a public meeting.

One afternoon soon after I arrived in to work as associate editor in that stuffy little office – it was probably during the printers' strike of 1952 which broke out almost as soon as I was installed – I was wading through a vast dusty mountain of submitted material, when I began to wonder if there were even more manuscripts in the drawer at knee-level. When I opened it, I found only one, fairly bulky, hand-written and dog-eared, with many revisions and some vicious stabbings out of whole paragraphs. I immediately recognised the handwriting. Peadar, meanwhile, had strolled in, and was casually looking through some galley-proofs hung up on the wall when I came across the following remarkable lines, not stubbed out anywhere, seeming to flow straight from brain to page:

An island is not like a glen. There is more sky over an island. The sea itself is like a turnover of the sky. There is more light on an island; inside and outside a house there is more light.

A young, newly married woman called Brigid is speaking, and when I asked Peadar about the manuscript he looked evasive, as any writer would. 'It's a thing I seem to have lost interest in,' he muttered. 'Probably I'll never finish it.' He went on to say that he had heard the story while he was on the run in Donegal and was being given shelter by a family whose mother used to sit up late at night chatting to her daughter-in-law.

What I remember about the longish silence that followed Peadar's words is a tram clanging by outside, but what I was actually thinking about at that moment were litter bins. Peadar had dreamed up a neat scheme to clean up Dublin just before I left for foreign parts. He would do this and raise funds for *The Bell* by making a small initial expenditure on the bins. He would then sell the space on those bins to commercial concerns and in no time at all his costs would be covered and the rest would go to help support the best literary magazine Ireland had ever had. I remembered hearing from friends who came over on visits how delighted Peadar had been with the success of his scheme.

'Peadar', I said to him with low cunning, 'it would be a very *untidy* thing to leave this novel unfinished.' He shrugged, picking up his famous grey hat with the crumpled brim, no doubt on his way over to Bewley's. 'Besides,' I continued, 'somebody else will finish it after you're dead. O'Flaherty maybe. Or even some young opportunist, more likely, whose contributions you wouldn't even use, but who might talk some publisher into going with the idea. Sure I might even flog the idea myself. Think of *Edwin Drood* – does anybody *really* know who finished that when Dickens at last fell off his perch? An unfinished novel is a *dangerous* thing for a writer to leave behind – a sort of loose cannon.'

Peadar gave me an astonished and indignant look from his extraordinary blue eyes before he plonked on the hat and was gone. About three weeks afterwards I noticed that the manuscript was gone too and three years after that again, when even *The Bell* was gone, *The Big Windows* came out in London in 1955 to high critical praise.

Whatever the circumstances in which Peadar finished that novel, it was a good one, of which any writer could be proud, and It is a novel that brings the reader close again to the territory that O'Donnell and O'Flaherty made peculiarly their own: men and women pitted against the elements, trying to make a life worth living out of scrubland, rock and sea and their own ceaseless labour. O'Donnell's young Brigid, who feels threatened by the darkness of the glen when she remembers the melting light flowing all over her island, is one of the most appealing of all his characters – strong, resourceful, friendly and ultimately successful in her life.

Those qualities were in Peadar too, allied to a stubbornness that made the going not always easy. He was not only a novelist who hated to write, he was an editor who, as I discovered over many months, wanted no part whatever in the actual editing process. However, selection was apparently a different matter. Occasionally he would breeze in and inquire, 'What have we coming up for next month, child?' He would nod his head in approval over regular contributers whom he had recruited years before, people like John Hewitt, Michael Farrell or Padraic Fallon. About new writers, particularly of fiction, he could be cautious, and one day his eye fell on a short story by a new young writer who soon afterwards definitively proved himself at the house of Macmillan. Peadar's method of gutting something was to let his eye travel rapidly along the galley proof while it was still hooked to the wall. He turned over, and read a few sentences of the next galley. Then he shook his head.

'Won't do at all. Won't do at all, childeen.'

The double diminutive was enraging, in the circumstances, but I held my cool. Did he realise that the story had been formally *accepted* before I had sent it to the printers? He had, after all, handed over full editorial responsibility to me when he hired me. This request was highly unethical, and another thing: had he considered the effect on the young writer? It was, by the way, a story with an authentic rural setting, but its tone was urban. It was a time in Ireland when Peasant Quality, P.Q. as the Abbey called it, was still high on the criteria list for good writing. For instance, in certain quarters, Elizabeth Bowen and Kate O'Brien tended to be dismissed as 'alien to the real traditions of this little country', but not formerely in *The Bell*.

'*All* fertility comes from the land, child' said Peadar mysteriously. That was one of a few occasions when I offered my resignation, although in this instance, everything was resolved amicably enough over coffee in Bewley's. Unless goaded beyond my limits, I could not really afford to throw up that job at the time and *he* made some conciliatory noises about the unlikelihood of his being moved to disagree again. I challenged him about whether he wanted to be an active editor again or not, and he made a joke of it. We left it at that.

To be fair, lack of interest in a good new writer was a rare thing for Peadar. He had always been on the lookout for people who not only could write well but who chose to write sociologically, for want of a better word. I'm thinking of people like James Plunkett, Donal Mac Amhlaigh, Brendan Behan and of course Patrick Kavanagh, parts of whose *Tarry Flynn* had first appeared in the pages of *The Bell*.

Some of Peadar's swans were undoubtedly geese who hissed a great deal, and sometimes tried to bite the hand that fed them, but he was always kind and supportive, and ever willing to part with money. In fact, Peadar O'Donnell could be regarded as a One Man Arts Council, functioning tangentially to the real one, at a time when literary prizes were few and far between, and when Aosdána was decades into the future. He was certainly arbitrary in his favours but nobody who knew him doubted his sincerity or his great affection for the underdog.

On Fridays, for instance there was usually a short queue of Peader's "private pensioners" waiting at the office door for their ten shillings, and Peadar passed on this charitable habit to one of my predecessors, Harry Craig, who in the late nineteen forties was nearly always in the office, whereas Peadar might have departed with his family for the weekend to Donegal. Harry's salary of £5 a week must have been under severe stress at times, but he was philosophical about it: 'There, Val, but for the grace of God...' he said it to me one Friday after the last pensioner had gone clattering off happily down the stairs. Ten shillings would buy that pensioner a night's drinking.

The thing about Peadar was that his example did tend to rub off on those around him. When you were in his company, you tended to see needy people in a different way, less as individuals than as members of a community which had somehow, and against all the rules, let them down. *'Fe scath a cheile a maireann na daoine'* (It's in the shelter of one another that people live) is a concept he believed in profoundly, and the theme of a remote rural community supporting one another by the means of the *meitheal* informal unpaid work-unit during the spring-sowing, hay-making, and harvest time, runs through many of his books. It used to be the only method of survival and, according to O'Donnell's biographer, Michael McInerney, Peadar spent many fruitless years trying to mould the IRA into a 'living social force'. He and friends like George Gilmore, Seán Murray and Frank Ryan saw national freedom as a means to social revolution and not as an end in itself.

When I read McInerny's book a few years ago, I understood why a man I had always taken to be anticlerical frequently pointed out to me that people got the priests they deserved. I don't know how he would have modified this in the context of sadistic clerical ravishers of children, but revelations about *them* were decades away. Peadar used to say that it was the people who subtly directed the priests, and not the other way around. I found this novel view particularly irritating when he insisted on cutting out some fine fiery paragraphs I had written about Father Daffy, Parish Priest of Roscrea, who took money in advance from Annie D'Alton and then refused, on the grounds of indecency, to let her put on in the parish hall a play called *A Priest in the Family* by Kieran Tunney - which of course he had neither seen nor read. It turned into one of the Famous Fusses of those years when the unfortunate Protestant Rector agreed to rent *his* hall, not knowing of the Father Daffy involvement. Peadar sent me on assignment to verify the story, and then attempted to emasculate my copy when I got back. That was another occasion when I came close to resigning.

The thing was he refused to have Father Daffy shown up in his true colours on the grounds that the 'poor man' had a very conservative parish! The poor man, as it happened, took off for Rome like a bat out of hell as soon as the thing became a *cause célèbre* and, although he was back home when I arrived in Roscrea, he refused to see me.

It's taken me about forty years to understand something of what was behind Peadar's extraordinary volte-face. It seems that, while on the run during the Civil War, he received a lot of help, which kept him alive, from country parish priests, for whom he retained a great affection. Stranger still, he even refused to condemn gombeen men. He used to argue that they were the only bankers the people had and they could not have stayed in business without charging interest! One hundred per cent interest?

Peadar O'Donnell is a man I knew well for only a few years, and I have reason to be grateful to him for allowing me to work flexi-time before that horrid term was invented, but I never understood the complexity of the man. Nevertheless, even when I was most annoyed with him, over things like rejecting an accepted contribution in galley proof, it was the sort of annoyance one feels for an exasperating father. Fortunately, he was for most of the month an absent father, although he may have come in some mornings while I was working on my novel at home.

It took me about six weeks' steady work to make any noticeable impression on that mountain of hopeful contributions, and in the process I excavated a few treasures. I found the earliest short stories of a writer called Richard Power, a tall fair young civil servant who had a fairly bad stammer and a sharp interesting approach to his rural settings. He was Waterford born, but from second level on had lived in Dublin with his family. His prose style was fresh and uncluttered, whether he was writing in Irish or in English, quite free of any romantic approach to the countryside.

After initial encouragement, Dick Power often dropped in to the office with new work, but nothing we published could have prepared anyone for the brilliant dark novel that emerged in 1966 called *The Hungry Grass*. He had married by then and spent, I think, two years, on leave of absence, from the Civil Service at the University of Iowa. His death from a heart attack, aged forty-two, when he was living outside Dublin again and the father of four or five young children, was a great blow to Irish literature, to his wife Anne, to those same children, and to dozens of us who counted ourselves his friends.

That small stuffy office in O'Connell Street could be a quite sociable place towards the end of 1952. James Plunkett worked just across the bridge in the Workers' Union of Ireland and he often dropped in, and indeed became a lifelong friend of mine. John Jordan would sometimes make a dramatic appearance, full of gossip about the *Hamlet* production which Mícheál Mac Liammóir and Hilton Edwards took to Elsinore in 1952. Edna O'Brien might appear offering more poetry, or Patrick Kavanagh might irrupt noisily into the office bellowing for his free copy of *The Bell*, or Denis Meehan might come over from the radio station with a couple of new poems and his latest collection of outrageous puns. I can remember too the gentleness and generosity of poet Valentin Iremonger and the sheer entertainment value of Christine Longford, who was as brilliantly witty when she climbed those stairs to deliver a book review as ever she was on paper, and Maurice Kennedy made everybody laugh over his troubles as one of the few bearded men around Dublin. That is, until another beard made its appearance – there is reason to believe that it belonged to Aidan Higgins who, as a Trinity student, had legitimately more time than Kennedy to air himself after morning coffee in St Stephen's Green. Maurice said that he himself was more than once called to account by the Chief Examiner of his Revenue office, which was just next door to the Country Shop. How was it that Kennedy's eleven o'clock coffee break at that establishment so often extended to almost lunchtime around the Duck Pond in the Green? Eventually other beards appeared to adorn the faces of Liam Miller, Tom Kinsella, Frank Barry (a young poet and architect) and several others, so Kennedy's troubles on that score were over.

Benedict Kiely always seemed to inhabit some trouble free zone far above everybody else. He was sunny with tolerance of the whole wide world, and remained so into old age, except perhaps for the bone-headed members of the Censorship Board, who had banned several of his novels. Also, from time to time, Basil Payne would appear, a Dublin poet who had a fine lyrical gift, and also the lightest of touches when dealing with Dublin street characters: like the man who cried 'Coal Blocks!' as he pushed around his handcart, the Glimmerman, Bang-Bang, Damn-the-Weather, and a variety of Dublin Jews who inhabited a part of Dublin known as Little Jerusalem, and were in the habit of paying neighbours' children to light the fire for them on the Sabbath. Payne is a legitimate chronicler of a vanished Dublin, and he has been almost completely sidelined by newer and, in some cases, inferior voices. He comes in a direct line from James Stephens, but you can search present-day anthologies and find never a trace of him.

One day I found, among the post, an open postcard addressed to me and I read it with some amazement: 'I stood in O'Connell Street the other day and looked up at what I thought was your office, before deciding I couldn't, after all, call in because I wasn't sure...'

It was signed F.O'C. and I was delighted to discover that the handwriting was the same as had come back to me when I had written to thank Frank O'Connor for his generous response to my first novel. Unprompted, he had spoken of it so enthusiastically to Carmel Snow, New York editor of *Harper's Bazaar*, that she had published some sections of it together with an introduction by O'Connor and a photograph of me by Cartier-Bresson. It was the luckiest break I had had to date, and I made more than twice as much money from it as from the novel itself. However, I had never met O'Connor, although I had admired his work for years, especially those wonderful loamy stories like 'The Long Road to Umera', and 'Uprooted', and 'Guests of the Nation'. One day I read a new short story of his called 'The Pretender' in the *The New Yorker* and I wrote to his home in England, asking if we could reprint it in *The Bell*. His reply came by return. He agreed to give us the story provided Peadar 'coughed up £7 for the UK and Irish rights' and provided that his revised copy of the story was used. His agent would send it to me.

I think I learned more from that handwritten postcard than in all my previous years of trying to write. I had always believed in the necessity for revision, but somehow it had never occurred to me that there was no end to that process, even in the case of a world famous fiction writer. The very idea that, apparently, what was good enough for *The New Yorker* (whose fees were believed in Ireland to be the highest in the world) was not good enough, after careful reassessment, for O'Connor himself stunned me. I compared the two versions, and the differences were minimal. But the revised story was sharper and better.

Years later when I made school visits for the Arts Council, that story of O'Connor's severity on himself went up and down the countryside, and to this moment I can recall the amazement on young aspirant faces as the implication sank in. The necessity for revision became my gospel to those schoolchildren, and I think it must have been news that would be applicable across the whole range of their studies. Today when I come across underworked and sloppy prose, and sometimes prize-winning underworked sloppy prose, I think of Frank O'Connor.

His great friend Seán O'Faoláin disagreed with O'Connor about a detail of the process. Seán believed that compulsive revision of youthful work in the case of reprints was bad because it was 'a kind of forgery'. His point was that an accumulation of years made you a different person to the one who wrote that story and so you were, in his view, messing about with the work of another writer.

All the same, O'Faoláin revised copiously as he wrote, certainly in the case of articles and editorials. His famous letter to the Bishop of Galway about his criticism of *The Bell* was criss-crossed with revisions, additions and subtractions to the extent that I wondered if the typesetters would ever make sense of it. They did, those Cahill gentlemen being well used to O'Faoláin over the years.

I was privileged to know Seán O'Faoláin reasonably well, and to enjoy his hospitality towards the end of his life – but sadly I did not meet Frank O'Connor, although I seemed to know him so well from his letters. I couldn't believe my misfortune when, one wintry Saturday evening, I got home from a hike in the Dublin mountains and found another note in my letterbox. 'Sorry I missed you again. F.O'C.' He had been visiting his friends the architect and writer Niall Montgomery and his wife Hop, and been told that I lived next door. He was leaving for the United States the next day, to work as visiting Professor somewhere or other. By the time he returned to live in Dublin, I was married to Maurice Kennedy and we had eventually finished redecorating our old house. I wrote inviting him and his wife Harriet to the housewarming, and he phoned back at once saying they'd be delighted to come if he was well enough – he was phoning from his sick bed. In fact, the big splendid voice didn't sound very strong any more, but I had no idea he was near the end of his life and that the time for meeting him had at last run out. I owed him so much. Even my job on *The Bell* was partly due to him. 'Frank O'Connor said you wrote a good book', said Peadar before he hired me. But he could be critical about my efforts too:

Dear Val,

I think that I am a sufficiently proved admirer of yours to say that I'd love to pull your hair out for your last story in *The Bell*. I never mind a bad story per se. I do mind good talent wasted on bad technique. Look at your story and take it asunder. A priest who is apparently a foot-fetishist falls in love with a more than usually attractive foot and conquers his temptation. An Irish boy – also apparently a foot-fetishist succumbs to the same foot. And you, who apparently have a divided mind about feet, parcel the one story up in the other, sit on the parcel and say to the reader: 'Would you mind telling me am I for or against feet?' You don't have to have a consistent attitude, but you should have an attitude – for the duration. Your inconsistency has simply taken form in a crazy pattern which you can't control and which makes nonsense of both your stories.

I assume, you see, that you do take your job seriously, not like ... who rationalises his own gross technical incompetence into 'It's only a matter of taste' and 'Anyhow a lot of people like it'. That sort of attitude is endemic to provincial towns. I have still not answered a letter from another Irish writer who has written what

124

he thinks is a brilliant short story and wants the name of someone on *The New Yorker* he can send it to. Of course the story is a masterpiece but it needs a handpicked reader – it's all a matter of taste.

Forgive the growl and come to see us if you are in London.

Frank O'Connor.

Looking back from this lifetime's distance, I find it incredible that I didn't go to London especially to see him and give him a good laugh over what I was not prepared to write down – I had at the time of writing never heard of a foot-fetishist! The story had been told to me in Florence, and the very organ-loft pointed out to me from which the young monk had fled, rather than have his eyes straying from the hands of his pupil to the suntanned bare foot in Greek sandals beside his own sandalled foot. Of course the mischievous girl (being a Florentine) had noticed his difficulty and always wore the same revealing sandals to her lesson. Before I heard the story, I hadn't thought of a foot as a legitimate object of desire. Maybe the curve of a breast behind a layer of thin cotton, or the fragile back of a beloved's neck, vulnerable and asking to be touched? But a foot? It seemed the devil tempted our young monk, and rather than touch it under the pretence of settling the foot properly in position on one of the organ pedals, he had fled down the ancient spiral staircase like a demented thing and never turned up for a lesson again. It was, of course, a very bad story which I had tried and failed to salvage and which I never included in any subsequent collection. We had good teachers in those old masters of the short story long, long ago. And I haven't yet stopped regretting that death robbed me of ever meeting one of them.

After Frank O'Connor's death in 1966, when I was preparing a radio tribute to him, I realised that if we had got to know one another, we would probably have disagreed as often as not. For instance, he often wrote one of his postcards complaining about this or that in a new issue of *The Bell*, and one of the contributions he most hated was something I was particularly chuffed to have succeeded in getting – extracts from Mícheál Mac Liammóir's diary during the Gate Theatre's tour of Denmark with their Elsinore production of *Hamlet*. I had seen a preview of it at the old Cork Opera House, and been bowled over by its scope and authority. I had to admit that this complex clever prince must have failed a remarkable number of exams if he was still in college at the age of fifty-two. Of course it mattered no more than did the age of the divine Sara Bernhardt when she brought her *Hamlet* to London in 1889. She was forty-five that year.

However, O'Connor was not just cranky about Mac Liammóir's *Hamlet*. He regarded the marvellous actor not only as a stage Irishman but (much worse!) as a phoney Corkman. The irony of that was that it took the rest of us another twenty-five years or so to find out that the man who spoke and wrote the Irish language more naturally and much more beautifully than anybody else north, south or east of Connemara was in fact the grown-up child actor called Alfred Lee Willmore, born in the county of Middlesex on 25 October 1899, and residing from infancy at the home of his parents, 150 Purves Road, Kensal Green, London SW10. There is a little pen drawing of that respectable Victorian house made in the course of his researches by Christopher FitzSimon and reprinted in his valuable and delightful biography, *The Boys* (1994).

I learned the startling truth of Mac Liammóir's nationality only a few years earlier when I read Micheál Ó hAodhá's *The Importance of Being Micheál* (1990) more than a decade after the actor's death. One of the epigraphs Ó hAodha uses, from Michael Holroyd's three-volume biography on Shaw, is the sort of apologia Mac Liammóir might have used himself if challenged: 'I believe that while we are alive we lie to protect ourselves from the truth itself. The lies we tell are part of the life we lead and therefore part of the truth.'

I shall never know now whether Frank O'Connor knew the truth or not – it's possible that he felt it, I suppose. But I understand that a few of Mac Liammóir's colleagues and friends did know he wasn't Irish, but chose not to talk about it. Did Hilton Edwards, his partner in two senses for all those years, know that Mícheál was as English as he was himself? I have no idea, but I have an abiding memory of one of the tenderest moments I have ever witnessed between two men.

I called in on them one wintry Saturday in Harcourt Terrace in 1974 to collect an introduction which Mícheál had written, at my request, for a book I was editing. He opened the hall door himself, clad in pyjamas, a red silk Chinese dressing gown slung over one arm and a big smile on his face. "Come in, my dear, come in." He walked with the carefulness of the almost blind, and ushered me in to his downstairs bedroom, a room that Beardsley might have designed: yellow curtains framing bare black trees, a tall rectangular tapestry on one wall, books lining another, a plumed fan above his bed, an antique screen to shut out the draughts. He got back into bed and motioned me into a chair beside it and then he began to talk, the large black eyes, which used to be so brilliant, fixed vaguely in my direction. He talked about the actress Ria Mooney and her time with them at the Gate, and I told him that there had been a reported sighting of the Grey Lady at the theatre the night Ria died – had he heard that? He hadn't but he wanted to know if I had heard about another Gate ghost, the ghost of Dom Bowe, a stage carpenter who had killed himself in the nineteen thirties. I hadn't, but at this point Hilton breezed cheerfully in, kissed my hand with his usual gallantry and asked why I never wrote about the theatre any more. I said because the editor paid me to write about television, and he said that television seemed to him to be what had replaced the Roman Circus – one watched government ministers being chewed up by the interviewers as one used to watch Christians being devoured by lions.

But he had really come to ask Mícheál if they should phone for flowers to bring to their hostess that night. "Page two of the Telephone Directory, dear", beamed Mícheál and Hilton wandered off.

"Dom Bowe?" I prompted because I shared Mícheál's passion for ghost stories.

"I'll tell you about him in a minute." He wriggled in the bed and gestured in Hilton's wake. "You'll see, he'll be back. When two men live together, one of them is always the housekeeper, and when I'm laid up everything goes to pot – nobody knows *when* to do anything. Flowers, I ask you, at this time of night!"

Hilton trailed back, disappointed. The florist was shut. Never mind, he had a silly present for their hostess that would have to do. 'Trouble is, my dear,' [this to me], 'I run a six-day business for people who insist on a five-day week. Nobody does *anything* on a Saturday any more." His eyes fell on Mícheál's introduction which I had picked up off the bed, ready for my departure.

'Pardon me,' he said, taking the manuscript and skimming rapidly through it. 'Now, Mícheál, I'm not sure about this. 'She was not a liar' – I think even the denial is a bit strong. Do you have to say 'liar'?' Mícheál pulled a face and looked stubborn, then tried to solicit my support above Hilton's elephantine shoulders. 'Very well, then, Mícheál, very well. But you haven't *signed* it, dear, have you? Here's my pen. There. No, sit up properly and lean on *this*.'

That's the image I carried away with me as I walked home along the Grand Canal: that picture and the story of Dom Bowe which may fit into this book somewhere else. The picture was of Hilton gently bending over the bed and holding a writing block with the manuscript on top of it, at just the right angle for a man to sign whose eyes have almost totally failed him.

Mícheál wrote his name with a flourish, the pen held as though it were a stick of chalk between the long curling fingers, and Hilton said, "That's it. Now the date, Mícheál, Jan. 5th, 1974."

Mícheál leaned up to pull yet another face at me, *enfant terrible* to the last, although he was in fact the senior partner by about eighteen months.

Mícheál died four years afterwards in that same room, on 6 March 1978, and his lifelong partner survived him for four increasingly lonely years. The internationally famous theatre they founded in 1928 lives on as their fitting memorial.

Apart from O'Connor, there was another Cork writer and editor who must have spent many years of his life giving objective criticism and advice to the aspiring young. David Marcus had the reputation among us of sometimes writing longer letters of analysis than the work you submitted to him. Nobody knew for ages what he looked like because he seemed never to be found in Dublin. We suspected he was a kind-looking, and probably stooped, old gentleman who had put his life's savings into founding a literary magazine whose standards were sky high. Everybody approved of him because when he did publish your contribution he paid promptly for it, without endless requests for the fee and many wasted stamps. But the advantage of being published in *Irish Writing* was not only financial. You might find yourself listed on the green cover beside Hemingway, Seán O'Faoláin, Graham Greene, Elizabeth Bowen, or maybe William Saroyan or Frank O'Connor. You might be listed beside Arthur Koestler.

It wasn't until the autumn of 1953 (on our honeymoon in fact, driving a battered Morris 10 along the west coast from Cork to Mayo) that Maurice Kennedy and I met this kindly 'old gentleman' at last. We had both had work accepted by David and, at the last moment, fairly strapped for cash, we phoned to ask him if we could meet him in Cork to collect our cheques. He immediately agreed, and said he would meet us on Patrick's

Bridge at half-past three on 2 September. We thought this was the charming vagary of an old person to whom meeting people in pubs would not come naturally, but who didn't fancy the prospects of having his office invaded. We, of course, would have loved to see it!

Anyhow, nearing the half-hour, in a drizzle of fine rain, we stood scanning faces and slow-moving elderly people who crossed the bridge. Until he stopped beside us, exactly as Shandon bells were striking the half-hour, we didn't notice the dapper young man, about our own age, with his crop of curly black hair and his very white smile. In a ripe Cork accent he said, "You must be – " and we said together: "You can't be David Marcus!"

"Just the same, I am", he said, and handed us an envelope each after we had shaken hands. "I'm very sorry but I'm on my way to the printers, so I hope you'll excuse me."

"No time for a celebration drink on us?" said I, a bit disappointed.

"Or a quick coffee?" Maurice added, which, if David had agreed to anything, would have been closer to the mark.

"Next time you're in Cork I'll be delighted," he said, and then he gave us a huge smile. "Let me wish you long life and happiness together. There'll be other times to meet properly." We thanked him heartily for the good wishes, and the cheques. Another big smile and he was gone.

It was perhaps an unlikely beginning to a lifelong friendship, but that's how it was. Years later he married Ita Daly, the novelist and short story writer, and she became an equally close friend of ours.

Friendship as a basis for marriage was cemented between Maurice and me when tragedy unexpectedly invaded our honeymoon. In the beginning it was idyllic. The old car, heroically loaned to us by Denis McAuley, a Revenue colleague of Maurice's, burned a horrendous amount of petrol during the journey but brought us to Galway without any other protest. During our few days in the city, we saw a luminous performance of The Playboy of the Western World at the Taidhbhearc, with the unlikely duo of Siobhán McKenna and Cyril Cusack as the lovers. The old car then carried us across the bog to Roundstone and up along the coast to Achill. The car had given us no trouble, but it was because we and the owner had feared trouble that we planned to end our trip in Youghal where Maurice's father was ill in hospital.

One breezy morning we were lingering over The Irish Times after breakfast before going for our swim when the face across the table from me changed colour as he pushed the paper over to me. There on the back page was his father's name among the death notices. None of the family had known precisely where we were, and so this was the way Maurice had to learn. It was a moment of horror and remorse, but my husband was very calm and asked me to get our things together while he settled the bill (the Achill landlady refused to charge us a penny). I wanted him to phone his mother but he said there was no phone in the house, so we sent a telegram to say we were on our way to Youghal.

It was a strange journey. We never even thought of stopping for a meal, and mysteriously Denis McAuley's car seemed to understand that drinking and driving by turns on the way to Youghal was not on. She complained a bit on steep hills, but she didn't break down. Maurice spoke very little, except to ask me to light another cigarette for him – he smoked almost continuously all the way, but he did stop the car just once when the little town, the town where he was born, came in sight across the ferry from Monatrea. The old waterside houses were painted blue or white, and behind them the blackened medieval town walls and the bell tower of St Mary's Cathedral were haloed in the fading yellow hue of evening.

"It's beautiful", I said.

"Wait until you see it in morning light", Maurice said. I tried to hug him before he started up the car again but he said

"Don't" and it was then I realised the strain he must have been suppressing since breakfast. I lit another cigarette for him as we drove across the lovely old bridge which separated Cork from Waterford. Oil lamps were being lit in the small cottages as we drove into Youghal and a broad track of brilliant white light was flashing across the harbour from the lighthouse. It blinked, was gone, flashed, and blinked again.

The house of Maurice's grandparents was one of three or four tall late Georgian houses at the end of The Mall, directly facing the water. As we neared it, I saw two small women waiting in the spill of light from their open door. They ran forward as we neared the house, and Maurice's mother enfolded him even before he had stepped out onto the pavement. His Aunt Mina ran around to my side of the car, and she was so small that I had to bend down to receive her welcome.

I felt we were at fault for not going straight to Youghal, but Mam, as everybody called her, refused to hear of it. She told us that Michael was insistent, as his condition worsened, that Maurice was not to be told, and that none of the wedding arrangements was to be altered in the slightest way. I suspect that he died as he lived, accepting with grace whatever life brought to him, including his death. But I keenly felt the loss of a single handshake or glance of recognition from Michael Kennedy, the father of my husband, and I went on feeling that until the three grandchildren he never saw were well grown, with children of their own.

That night in a room overlooking the harbour, which had been Maurice's room on childhood holidays, he cried salt tears for the loss of his father, and so did I.

10

Rus in Urbe

Rathgar in 1953 was in a time warp, if only we had known it. The broad and beautiful main road was considered busy if three bicycles, and two or three widely separated cars could be seen along the whole wide leafy stretch of it. It was a place where the loudest sound in summer was the whirring of lawn mowers, and where country-born beggars like 'The Music Man' were greeted with cries of delight by small children who rushed indoors for pennies to push through the railings. 'The Music Man' was always dressed, winter and summer, in an old soft hat and what used to be called a 'dustcoat', a sort of light cotton raincoat with raglan sleeves which certainly wouldn't keep out a light shower. His wide-legged flannel trousers and brightly polished worn black shoes were an indication of better days, and he played on his fiddle tunes like 'I Dreamt I Dwelt in Marble Halls', or 'The Old Bog Road', and nearly always ended with 'The Teddy Bears' Picnic', before coming over to the children, and then passing on to the next stretch of road.

He came to our tree-lined avenue every Monday, and sometimes if the children were playing in the back garden I would hear him first while I was snatching a breath of air under the beech tree before settling down to work. We would chat for a few minutes before I handed over sixpence, or, on lucky days, a shilling. He told me he used to play for regular dances in halls around the countryside and that he knew Val Vousdan well. Val was an old-style entertainer who gave 'recitations' and sang music-hall ditties or patriotic ballads for a living. I had heard of him because of my father. If I'd already started to work, and heard 'The Music Man' through the open window beside my desk, he never interrupted me by knocking at the door, but he would be given double pay the following week.

Peadar O'Donnell was unusual in that I wasn't sacked on marriage – he said that I could work on until the end of the year and then we'd see. By Christmas I was pregnant [that was the way of things then] and the job was extended until the birth of the baby. The novel, and the child we called Maev, appeared within two months of one another the following summer (1954), and that was the end, for many years, of my career in the workplace.

The next book of mine that I care to acknowledge didn't happen until 1978, although there were a couple of children's books in between which I didn't consider good enough. They were, however, translated into German by Elisabeth Schnach and published by Benziger of Zurich. But when André Deutsch brought out *Antiquities*, in 1978 and the publicity machine started to roll – it was quite a primitive piece of machinery then – the journalists who called seemed obsessed with one question. What had I been *doing* all those years since the publication of my second novel? The question always amused me, but it was quite hard to answer without appearing priggish. I was actually co-rearing three children at a time when play-schools and child-minders hadn't been invented, and if one did not have an extended family of grandparents, one needed a live-in nanny which was not financially possible for us. I remember at that time there were quite a few such nannies in Rathgar, wearing a grey or blue and white uniform, who wheeled out giant gleaming perambulators, with a small handsomely dressed child holding on at either side. One such nanny in due course had four children and an infant to care for, and she strolled along wheeling two infants with two toddlers riding on a little seat in front of her and a child of five or six spinning ahead on what was known as a 'fairy-bike'. I hardly knew the mother of all these children. She was understood to be *in business*, quite rare for a woman in the nineteen fifties.

Around about this time I became what was contemptuously known among the godly as an *à la carte* Catholic. The irrational authoritarian attitude of the Irish hierarchy, led by Rome, towards the only effective contraception of the time was something I decided to have nothing to do with. I went on *the pill*. Very properly my husband believed such a decision ought to be entirely at the discretion of the female. A lifetime afterwards, I find it astonishing that a male-dominated Rome is still promulgating futile sex laws which almost nobody now left, among churchgoing Roman Catholics, obeys.

I have no doubt that a more disciplined woman than I (once the decision about how many children were manageable had been made), would have incorporated a new novel into the schedule every couple of years, but it didn't happen. The fact is I found the work involved in bringing up three children a fascination. I loved teaching them to read. I loved reading to them in the dusky winter afternoons – Beatrix Potter, Kenneth Grahame, E. Nesbitt and the rest – and I loved taking them on longish walks along the towpaths of the river Dodder, and later, up into the Dublin mountains. We didn't own a car for quite a few years, and the children came out with us on the seats of our bikes to pick blackberries or for a paddle in Sandycove.

Later, when we acquired an ancient Morris 10, we used to go farther afield, to Trim, for instance, where we walked around the unprotected walls of the great Norman castle, or to the unrestored Newgrange when it was a large grassy knoll in the flat lands of Meath. You took a candle with you to examine the intricate carvings inside. I remember that the children at this stage were small enough to walk upright to the inner chamber, while Maurice and I had to stoop. Their father gave us the benefit of his theories about the lever system used to build this wonderful place, which he said was older than the Pyramids – and, a bit later on, the archaeologists agreed with him. What seems strange to me now, looking back, is that on those dark November weekends, calm and mild as April, we would be the only people in search of the caretaker who held the keys to Newgrange or Dowth or Knowth, and who also gave us a loan of the candles we sometimes forgot to bring. We were almost always the only people inside the chambers and this is what the grown children seem to remember best. These secret ancient places seemed to belong to us because we claimed them.

Now with the advent of mass culture, and travel for all by television, the most famous archaeological sites in the world – Knossos, for instance, or Pompeii, or Lascaux – have suffered considerable damage from the summer hordes of sightseers, who have as much right to see such marvels as we had to bring in candle smoke, which may have stained the sacred carvings of Newgrange. Or as little right, depending on how you look at it.

Sometimes on these expeditions we had friends of the children squeezed into the back seat and usually they all sang on the way home: songs popularised by the Clancy Brothers or the Dubliners and scout songs like 'If you're happy and you know it clap your hands'. But one summer Ernest Gebler stayed with us for a few weeks, and taught the children melancholy spirituals like 'All my Troubles Lord', or merry ones like the tale of Little Moses found in the bulrushes, and black and beautiful ballads that the children knew but couldn't have understood, like 'The Four Marys', or the English ballad about the young hunter who shot his love down by the river because she was wearing a white apron and he took her for a swan. But why, one of the children wanted to know, would he want to kill a beautiful swan? 'Why do you want to eat dead

136

animals?' Ernie shot back, and even then I hoped he wouldn't put them off meat. He didn't, but he turned them permanently in the direction of good songs.

The children had an influence on Ernie too. At the time, after the break-up of his second marriage, to Edna O'Brien, Ernie could be said to be suffering withdrawal symptoms from the company of children. He spent long hours during that holiday with ours, and he taught them a variety of practical skills. They adored him. He instituted, to our amazement, a happening which was created to occur when the decibels at the back of the car ascended to an uncomfortable level.

This was known as 'Ernie's One-Minute Silence Period' and Ernie would announce it casually as though he were a radio announcer telling us what the next programme would be. There would be instant silence in the back of the car and sometimes during that minute our youngest child would fall asleep. When the period ended, the older children would be requested not to wake up their little brother by speaking too loudly, and so the official silence period was acknowledged to be over. Psychologically, it was a perfect device and it was adopted and lasted long after Ernie had gone home. It was only necessary to say in a conversational tone, 'Now we'll have Ernie's Silence Period' and there would be one or two reminiscent giggles before the silence.

Who really was Ernest Gebler? Sadly, it's probably necessary to explain to anybody under forty that Ernie became known in Dublin as the author of a striking first novel called *He Had My Heart Scalded*. The book was funny, it was touching, it dealt with the poverty that conceals poverty, and it was fizzing with promise. Real fame and fortune (particularly in America) came in 1953 with the publication of *The Plymouth Adventure*, an historic novel of great integrity which was beautifully written and thrilling to read, although, as Ernie proudly pointed out to us, he invented nothing whatever of the *Mayflower* story, but stuck scrupulously to journals and source material. The movie version which followed starred Spencer Tracy and was hugely successful.

Like Scott Fitzgerald, Ernie then tried script-writing in California for a while, but fell foul of McCarthyism. He returned to Ireland. There followed some work that didn't really seem to be Ernie at all, and in a tongue-in-cheek letter to Maurice he said: 'Forgive me for knocking off things which make money; it's a bad habit which I got from being poor in Dublin.'

In fact, it was the good work which made money and the next stage of Ernie's fame came in the nineteen sixties with a series of television plays which made him, if not exactly a household name, then at least a fashionable and highly praised darling of the English critics. *Call Me Daddy* is the sort of wickedly subversive and hilarious play that Shaw might have written, had he lived to be lured into the realms of television. It won a coveted *Emmy* award in 1968, and it starred Peter Sellers with Fionnuala Flanagan, a newcomer at the time, whose name Maurice Kennedy suggested.

Never wasteful, Ernie turned the script into a novel called *Shall I Eat You Now?*, the funniest novel in my opinion since Evelyn Waugh's *Scoop*. Gebler was living in London at this time and tended to be regarded as English because most of his settings were English. But Ernie was Irish to the bone, despite his Czech/Jewish father, and soon after the inauguration of Aosdána, he was rightly elected a member. He was living in Dalkey, just outside Dublin, by then, but he remained by choice an outsider whose voice was seldom heard at meetings.

The Ernie that I and my family remember with such affection was very different. He was buoyant company, and loved the countryside, trees, old houses, Ireland, music and children in about equal proportion. He was a shrewd judge of antiques and gleefully practised one-upmanship in acquiring beautiful things he wanted. Auctioneers, even of houses, would all go out of business if they were depending on Ernie. He once sold his house in London by beckoning into it would-be (but disappointed) buyers of a house just up the road from his own.

However, he could be generous to a fault with his friends. In our house a lovely late Georgian chest of drawers is referred to still as 'Ernie's chest', because he left it as a present after a few weeks' holiday with us at a lonely juncture in his life. Happily, a couple of years later, he followed us up to the Fanad peninsula in Donegal to introduce us to a beautiful young English partner. They set up house together some time afterwards and lived happily in Dalkey for at least twenty years, before Jane's tragically sudden death while doing the first of the spring jobs in her own garden. Soon after this, Ernie wrote us a long letter which we rightly identified as the onset of Alzheimer's Disease. He was a benign, silent, almost unknowable presence whenever I visited him in Dalkey or, later, in his Killiney nursing home. One day, searching for some way to crack the one-sided conversation, I mentioned that I had just heard a radio review of his son Carlo's new book.

'He's a good novelist, Ernie. Maybe a very good novelist.'

'Is he?' he said. '*Is* he?'

Ernie's slightly bent head had shot up, and the brown sunken eyes had brightened to look like the real Ernie's eyes once again. His pleasure was unmistakable, but it lasted only for a minute before that cruellest of human afflictions removed all expression from his face once more. When I was leaving, however, he did something quite characteristic of Ernie, although I knew he didn't remember who I was. He lifted both hands and slowly traced the outline of my head from crown to chin. I took this, with the formal farewell kiss, to be permission to visit him again, and it's one of the many regrets of my life that I couldn't face seeing again the blank shell which represented all that was left of our brilliant friend Ernest Gebler.

Saturdays. It's Saturdays I remember best when trying to piece together our lives in that unforgotten house behind the beech tree.

On Saturdays Doyle came to do odd jobs in the house and garden, and he was one of a dozen or so such men who were employed on a weekly basis to lend a hand in the running of those large Rathgar gardens all around us. They had been planned by, and were usually maintained by, the gardening enthusiasts who owned them, with just this minimum of help from jobbing gardeners. Most of the back gardens in our district had wonderfully productive fruit trees, King William pears, old varieties of Irish apple, plum and cherry trees. Usually there was no formal lawn, but often there were circular rose-beds between the trees and, in our case, a profusion of self-perpetuating spring bulbs scattered at random under the bare branches.

From late January we had waves of snowdrops, crocuses, dwarf irises brilliant in the depths of their blue, jonquils and daffodils and hyacinths along the length of the back garden – you could smell these flowers from any open back window. Later on in the year came wild primroses and shrubs like forsythia and barberis, taking over from winter jasmine and always, in the front garden, this nameless dark green feathery 'heather tree' as we called it – straggly and unattractive and almost unnoticeable until some warm April or early May night. Then, as you rounded the corner into our avenue from the Rathgar Road, your senses were seduced by this invisible cloud of perfume, strong, wild, all-pervading. Passing strangers sniffed and said 'What's that?' and may well have thought the gardens along our avenue were cross-patched with clumps of perfumed exotica. In fact, the neighbours were equally baffled. We knew because Miss Nisbet had explained all about the 'heather tree', although my memory is that even she could not put a correct botanical name on it.

It's probably the time to explain now that Miss Nisbet was our landlady, the last remaining member of the family who had left her this house. A tall, straight-backed and reserved American cousin of theirs, she had come first as a shy young girl in her late teens to spend a holiday with them, and later after the break up of her parents and her father's remarriage. She was happiest of all in the garden. Each of the family became devoted to her. Her name, Consuelo, was strange and she herself could never account for it. They called her 'Totsey', which was hilariously inappropriate, especially to us since we knew her only as a tall and graceful old lady, with striking eyes and a quiet, beautiful speaking voice.

When we got to know her better, she told me that, up to the late nineteen forties, she and one of the Miss Carrolls ran a private preparatory school in Dundrum, which provided a little garden for every child. During that time they became friends with Lily and Lolly Yeats, Jack and W.B Yeats' sisters in the village. Lilly had given her two of her father's books, which are among my own most treasured books now. The inscriptions typify the dignified remoteness with which even very good friends treated one another. Miss Elizabeth wrote, in a strong and rather dashing hand, on the title page of *Essays Irish and American* (published jointly by the Talbot Press and T. Fisher Unwin of London):

To Consuelo Nisbet
from Elizabeth Yeats
Summer 1924

And Miss Nisbet wrote for me when I asked her:
To Val Kennedy
From Consuelo Nisbet
July 1957

The little volume is handsome, printed on thick cream paper with capitals ornamented in the Celtic style, but what makes it a touching gift is that it was probably handed down from the owner's own shelves. Her personally designed bookplate decorates an endpaper, black and white and elegantly Art Nouveau. No *Ex Libris*, for some reason. Just Elizabeth Corbet Yeats, sturdily cut as though in stone under those little trees that recall Beardsley and which shelter a slender young woman in a cloche hat.

The John B.Yeats essays, mostly new to me at the time, are didactic and very typical. I particularly loved, from my first reading of it that day under the apple trees, his defence of Synge's *The Playboy of the Western World*. I knew that William Butler Yeats had supported Synge with equal passion when the rabble rose up against him in the Abbey Theatre, in 1904:

> 'Because of this enjoyment of the spectacle of life we have produced the ablest dramatists of latter-day England: Farquhar, Goldsmith, Sheridan, Oscar Wilde, G.B.Shaw. And of these Synge, though he died so young, is the greatest. He stands apart from them all because he portrays peasant poetry and passion and a humour which cuts deep into the mystery and terror of life ... Those who object to Synge's plays are suffering from the delicate stomach of people who have lived effeminate lives. Dr Swift would have come to Synge's plays and applauded them.'

And then a few pages farther on, there was this marvellous passage which told me that the old man had actually known Synge ('And did you not see Shelley plain?'). It must be remembered that we are talking about the 1950s. Synge was forty years dead, but Yeats and Joyce had died only about ten years previously, and the great prose writers Seán O'Faoláin, Frank O'Connor, Kate O'Brien, Benedict Kiely, Mary Lavin and Elizabeth Bowen were still very much alive. Jack Yeats, too, was still alive, and just drawing towards his greatest period of appreciation among his peers. I never missed an exhibition of his at Victor Waddington's gallery in South Anne Street.

Anyhow, the passage in John B. Yeats's book which fascinated me was this one:

> Synge's history was peculiar. He took up music as his profession and studied it in Germany, Rome and Paris; and having only a very small income, for economy's sake, always lived with poor people. In Paris he stayed with a cook and his wife who was a couturière. He told me that they had but one sitting room in which the man did his cooking and the wife her sewing, with another sewing woman who helped. When, as sometimes happened, a large order for hats came in, Synge, who by this time had given up music for philology, would drop his studies and apply himself to hat-making, bending wires etc. After a year or so, he moved into a hotel where he met my son who urged him to leave Paris for the West of Ireland.

When I re-read that passage today, I'm back under the swelling apple trees in that summer garden whose only sounds are sleepy birdsong and distant lawnmowers. My daughter is busy in her sandpit, only occasionally requiring my presence for consultation. On just such another day, an astonishing thing happens. Miss Nisbet materialises at my elbow wearing her canvas gardening apron and thick leather gloves and says, 'May I disturb you, Mrs Kennedy?', in that friendly and gentle voice. By this time she and Maurice and I and her cook-housekeeper Rose have become the best of friends, and instead of having just the front garden under the beech tree to sit and read and work in on sunny days, as we have by contract, we have this long beautiful back garden too. Miss Nisbet has judged the front garden to be too dangerous for a little girl who might be tempted to chase a ball on to the road. Our tree-lined avenue at this stage had about two or three elderly resident motor cars and the occasional horse and cart delivering coal blocks or logs.

Now, although our landlady and Maurice and I had been for six or seven years more like close friends than people with a business arrangement, we addressed one another formally as people of different ages did then, and we did not assume intimacy even when we occasionally entertained one another to supper in the evening.

'Won't you sit down, Miss Nisbet?' I said. The striped canvas chairs were hers to sit down on or not as she pleased but she was an old lady, probably more than twice my age, and for the first time ever I thought she looked tired. So I sped across the lawn to the apple house to fetch her a chair, and I sat down on the dry golden grass at her feet as she began to speak.

'I don't know if I'm going to surprise you too much, my dear. I hope not, but for a little while now I've been thinking about selling this house.'

If a bomb had dropped between us on the grass, I couldn't have been more shocked. Our roomy sunny apartment (half of this rather large house) had been *meant* for us. I knew it as soon as I stepped in to the place – it was on a Friday – and I begged Miss Nisbet to hold it until Maurice's free afternoon. In those days, civil servants worked five and a half days a week and so had only Saturday afternoon and Sunday free. I well remembered this friendly stranger's smile - I suppose my eagerness must have seemed a bit childish.

'Is this gentleman your husband?'

'He will be on the thirty-first of August', I said. This was June.

She smiled again. 'I won't make any decision until you both come together tomorrow.'

'Thank you *very* much.'

There was nothing like the same pressure on rented accommodation then as now, but of all the flats I had vetted, this was the only one I couldn't wait to show Maurice. Most of the other offers which I'd written into my notebook had turned out to be gloomy or damp or grubby or too far out of town or too small or too large, and the rest were too expensive. We could afford a maximum of ten pounds a month and this Rathgar flat was *perhaps* within our reach. Maurice, not being an optimist, thought we probably wouldn't get the place if it was half as nice as I had said.

The next afternoon we arrived on our bikes. This was an avenue of beech trees which predated the mid-Victorian houses, and in this sultry June weather the leaves had just passed their late spring glory of young green. They hung heavily now, casting shapes in dark shadow on the paving stones. There were a few whirring lawnmowers and a dog barking somewhere, but mostly profound silence. It might have been the heart of the country.

Number Thirteen slept behind its particularly fine beech tree, shadows of leaves freckling the tall windows. The twelve granite steps threw out the odd flash where the sun was catching an edge of mica, and Miss Nisbet was bent over the rockery with a trug half-full of flowers cut for the house.

She stood up to greet us and we shook hands. Then out of her canvas pocket she handed Maurice the key. The main hall door would be our private entrance, she said, and at the end of the upper hall was a small flight of steps with a locked door. Everything inside that little door would be ours.

'Wander around as you please up there and get the feel of the house. That will tell you whether or not the apartment is for you.' She smiled very warmly from one to the other of us and asked us to come later to the side door under the steps, and have a cup of tea with her, if we had time. She would enjoy that, she said.

We couldn't believe our luck as we wandered about the sunny empty spaces, which smelled of new paint and old wood. On one side of the hall was a drawing room running the entire length of the house, a faded hawthorn branch brushing against the back window. On the other side of the hall was a small square living room, and I pointed out where we could build bookshelves. A door opened from this to a small kitchen with a tiled fireplace. The second right-hand door from the hall opened on to a bathroom sparkling and new, and a beautiful little staircase outside this door led to what would be our bedroom. This big room had a slightly sloped attic ceiling and was brimming with light from the back garden. A very long back garden. Apple trees, a gnarled and twisted pear tree, old stone walls covered with climbing roses, and at the end of the garden a distant view of the dark blue Wicklow mountains and, much nearer, the spire of Christ Church, Rathgar. An old black cat was washing himself on top of a nearby outhouse.

I looked confidently at Maurice, who was shaking his head, 'Forget it. We won't be able to afford it,' he said. 'Not a chance!'

'But the ad said, 'Rent by negotiation'. Please let me handle it, Maurice. You needn't say a word until we see how it goes.'

He shrugged, then smiled with pity at me. We sat down on the bare but warm staircase while I explained my optimism.

'There are twelve ads copied from *The Irish Times* in the back of this notebook. I've looked at every one of them and you've seen about four, even including this. The cheapest of them costs about a tenner, and the rest are £12 or even £14. Most of the places are grotty or downright dirty and would need months of hand-scraping. Several of them are miles and miles out of town, but with hardly a tree in sight. This house is not only beautiful and spotless, in a lovely avenue of trees, but my feeling is that it will cost about the same as the rest, and it's in ten minutes' cycling distance of town.'

'I don't think you're right,' Maurice said, 'but go ahead if you think you can handle it.' Even then, as right through the rest of our lives together, he hated bargaining over anything – a piece of old furniture, deliberately priced for bargaining, a dodgy old car, a book, a picture, a pitchfork, anything. If he could afford the first-named price, he bought it, and if not, he walked away.

Downstairs, in Miss Nesbit's quarters it was less bright than upstairs, but lovely. The long low dining room was full of flowers and greenish light from the garden, and there was tea laid out for us on a small mahogany table. A large long-haired black cat – the one we had looked down on from the bedroom window – was sitting on the green hearthrug, staring at us.

'Pickles,' Miss Nisbet introduced him. 'Not very sociable, I regret to say.' She didn't know Maurice at the time, but Pickles did. He walked over stiff-legged and sat on the rug at Maurice's feet, still staring up into his face. Maurice casually stroked him on the head, and the caress was graciously accepted. 'I must confess that's a surprise to me', our hostess said as she poured the tea. It was she who told me years later that the Chinese, when entertaining a visitor, never continue a former topic of conversation if the subject happens to be serious. While drinking tea together, the subject of conversation must be light-hearted or humorous. It must signify a restful interval in any discussion, especially about money. Apart from Pickles, I don't remember what we did talk about, but I think there must have been a reference to the covered silver dish of hot scones that Rose brought in from the oven. Rose, who was small and squat and not much younger than Miss Nisbet, wore a white lacy cap and apron, and a dark blue long-sleeved dress. With a wicked smile at me, she flicked a tea towel at the still solemnly staring cat, who spat furiously at her and vanished through the door.

'I don't think that was very kind, Rose', Miss Nisbet gently reproved her maid, but clearly Rose was an independent spirit and she left the room smiling. 'There's an ongoing war between that pair', Miss Nisbet said, laughing heartily once the door had shut behind Rose.

'Poor Pickles', said Maurice.

It's a strange thing but I truly believe that cat would have made all the difference, if there had in fact been any difference, between us.

'We were just hoping before we came down', I eventually said, 'that we'll be able to afford your beautiful flat. We loved it as soon as we set eyes on it.'

'Did you have any sum in mind that you'd be comfortable with? Getting married is an expensive business I'm told.'

'We were thinking of £10 a month', I said.

'And a two year lease', said Maurice.

'That will suit me perfectly', said the wonderful woman at once. 'You see I know very little about the business of renting, but after my cousins died and left me this house I realised that dividing it was a way of being able to go on living here.'

'You could probably get a lot more for a splendidly spacious flat like that', Maurice said. This was entirely in character for him.

'Perhaps, but I would have to be happy about my tenants, and I think we shall all get along splendidly together. I needn't even ask Pickles about *you*, Mr Kennedy!'

And so, miraculously it was fixed before we left the house. The details of the contract were arranged between our solicitors. The flat was ours.

All that had been almost seven years earlier. We had three children now and, although we had made some attempt at house-hunting, so that they could each have a room to themselves, we'd really made no decision. Always the comparison between this well-loved house and the sort of place we could afford to buy held us back from a decision. My father had died and left me his own little house. When I sold it, there was enough left to share with my two brothers, and to buy a mortgage and a house for Maurice and me if we found the right one. It is probably true that we were *not* looking very seriously, and it's perfectly true that, left to Maurice, we would have found a house before long. He said he didn't care where we lived but he wanted me to be happy about any move. And so the years after the renewal of our lease wore on, and the only thing we attempted to change – or rather Maurice did

– was the rent. He said ten pounds wasn't enough, but Miss Nisbet reminded him she was the best judge of that. She and Rose adored the children. Pickles, even in advanced old age, climbed high walls to get away from them.

I was conscious, in the silence of the garden, of that moment before a storm. The house was about to tumble about our ears. I listened again in my head to the incredible words, 'for a little while now I've been thinking about selling this house. I know, after all, that you two are going to need more space as the children grow, and I know I shall never let the house again. It's been such a happy and successful time, but Rose and I are not getting any younger ....'

She had let her voice drift into silence and I felt like a dreamer who has missed a step on a long flight of stairs.

'When must we go?'

'Not a moment before you are perfectly suited, my dear. I think you both know that.'

'Thank you. I think we do.'

'When you discuss it with Maurice' – she had never used his first name before – 'you may find that the news will not be entirely fresh to him. He enclosed that little note with his cheque last month, remember?'

'What little note?'

Miss Nisbet hurriedly gathered together a few garden tools and stood up. 'Ask him this evening, my dear, won't you? And forgive me for assuming.'

'There's nothing to forgive. Maurice often does this sort of thing and then says 'Oh, didn't I tell you?' If I ever murder him, it will be for that. He shouldn't be surprised because he's often mentioned that, statistically, murder is a domestic crime.'

She went away smiling but, I could see, a little shocked by my joke.

Alone again in the sunny garden, it was impossible for me to settle into any sort of calm. By the time the boys returned, riotous after their day out with a friend, I had done hardly any work. In fact I had wasted a lot of time composing what I would say to Maurice. It might be of some interest to explain something of what I could understand myself of this complex man with whom I had already spent eight years of my life and was in fact to spend more than thirty years more.

The 'New Man' hadn't yet arrived on the scene in Dublin and when he did, some time towards the end of the nineteen sixties, nobody laughed louder than Maurice or made wickeder jokes about his aprons, his shelf of cookery books, and his stockpot. Yet although he himself couldn't (and wouldn't) boil an egg, he had been helping out with his children for years. He enjoyed the shared chore of bath night, once they had emerged from the hazards of infancy, and in due course loved taking them out cycling or helping with their homework, even though this sometimes ended in tears. Coming from a long line of teachers in Kerry and Limerick, he had a brilliant mind and a great ambition to imbue in his children a love of mathematics. I well remember his daughter emerging in angry tears from one of these lessons. She said, 'The trouble is he explains too much. He *knows* too much.' In truth, he was an unconventional beautiful man holding down a conventionally good job for the sake of his family. Once, before I met him, because he was affronted at being asked to repeat an oral Irish exam – his Irish was in fact very good – he started selling off or giving away his books, his racing bike and his Jelly Roll Morton records, and then he went to Belfast and applied to join the Merchant Navy. The Merchant Navy! Even then, they turned him down because of the state of his lungs.

Maurice's 'little note' had offered Miss Nisbet £2,400 should she ever consider selling her house. The hot summer wore on and it was she who began a search for a house and not ourselves. Predictably, because we had been her tenants for seven years, she decided that Maurice's offer was too high and she accepted it subject to a reduction of three or four hundred pounds - that was real money in those days when £2,400.00

150

would have been regarded as a very good bargain for a house like hers. Ultimately he beat her into accepting a smaller reduction. When, more than forty years later, I, widowed, was selling that house myself, I realised properly for the first time what it must have been like for Miss Nisbet to sell her home. She had never referred to the forthcoming removal in any but the most cheerful terms. Her house would be in good careful hands, she said. There would be the children, who had become her pets running about their own garden (we should, she said, build them a swing down near the old pear tree) and as for herself, the *burden* of that garden would be a pleasure to hand over to us. It was only when that garden became ours to maintain that we realised what she meant!

Miss Nisbet finally decided to buy a new house on the Rathfarnham Road with two small gardens. She was sensibly determined to allow herself the luxury of laying sods of grass, instead of seeding the ground, and so she would have two instant lawns, and maybe a few half-grown trees too. Her only worry about moving was Pickles. He was, she said, very old to change his ways, and she feared he would suffer. Rose told us cheerfully that the cat would probably have to be put down - she'd known cats here and there all her life, and cats didn't travel. We warned her not to mention this to Miss Nisbet, and one night Maurice went down and talked to this extraordinary woman who had, effortlessly, become one of our closest friends. He offered her any help he could give her about any aspect of the removal, and told her to phone him at any time day or night if any problem cropped up. He did not mention Pickles, but when he came up later he told me that he believed she knew precisely what problem might arise.

That first night when Miss Nisbet moved out, the house felt very strange, the downstairs part empty and echoing, but friendly just the same. We had a cellar now. We had a little larder full of shelves with a few jars of bottled pears left behind as a present, and a few pots of Rose's homemade jam. We had a broom cupboard and we had Rose's room across from the kitchen which would be perfect as a bedroom for the boys while they were small. We had a living room. We had a wash house. We had an apple house with sliding shelves and a wonderfully cidery smell from all the apple harvests of all the summers since 1870. We had a study. But, best of all, we had a back garden, shadowy now in the dusk with no cat meditating up on the wall, but with birds rustling in every tree. The roses were blurry in the dusk, and the big yellow one in its circular bed reached out as it always had, to touch one's arm. It smelled faintly of lemons.

Up in the pear tree a few song thrushes were settling down for the night, the winey smell of the ripening fruit no doubt like money in the bank to them. We stopped to watch two sparrows civilly await their turn for a last flutter in the birdbath, its level low now after the long hot day. I would refill it in the morning.

'You can't buy wild birds, and yet they are ours too', I said happily. 'All we have to do is feed them in the winter.'

'*And* bell the cat we are going to acquire without delay', Maurice said.

'Oh, of course.' The only rule we hadn't much liked about our tenancy was the ban on pets. Miss Nisbet had apologised for it, and said unfortunately Pickles wouldn't be able to tolerate opposition, even competition. He was too old.

The next morning we rang up to see how the new household had survived the night, and Maurice was so disturbed by what he heard that he drove to Rathfarnham right away. He had taken a few weeks' leave to coincide with the change-over. He found Miss Nisbet in a near enough to distracted state of mind. The old cat had howled all through the night, and on being let out by Rose that morning had vanished screaming into the woods behind the new housing estate. That had been four hours before. Pickles had neither eaten nor drunk anything since leaving the old house.

Maurice searched every nook and cranny of the small wooded wilderness and (no surprise to me) came back carrying the frantic cat restrained in his arms. They transferred him to the cat basket, and drove him to the local vet, Mr Lambert, who advised that he should be allowed to put the animal out of his misery. But Miss Nisbet and Maurice felt that Pickles should be given another day or two to settle, and they took him home again. Pickles spat defiance through the bars of the basket and left a trail of blood behind when Maurice suggested they try the ancient remedy of buttering the cat's paws in order to stop it from wandering. He came home shaking his head, saying the problem was beyond him, but he would leave it until the next morning. Who knows, if the cat responded to the taste of butter, he might well have settled by the time his paws were licked clean. But sadly, it didn't happen.

The following morning, the old cat, still refusing food and drink, was barely alive and there was only one further thing to be done. Maurice advised Miss Nisbet not to come when he drove Pickles to the vet for the second time. Injecting water into him was no good and he was dead within half an hour, stiff and bedraggled, with chunks of his lovely coat torn off and lying around him in his basket. He was buried in a corner of the new garden, and Maurice advised his grieving mistress not to come out until the job was over. Submissive as to a parent, although Maurice was the right age to be her son, Miss Nisbet stayed indoors.

After the first death there is no other? We buried four or five cats of our own in the back garden over the next forty years and it never became any easier. Pickles lived on in family folklore, and even to this day I never hear a heavy saucepan crashing on a tiled floor but I remember that same sound travelling up through the house when we lived upstairs. Whenever Pickles annoyed Rose too much (perhaps begging her for fish while she was cooking it), she deliberately let a heavy saucepan lid fall to the stone floor, which made him flee through the kitchen window as though pursued by demons. Poor Pickles, the only victim of the otherwise painless change in the ownership of number thirteen, Garville Avenue.

11

Making It Our Own

One night we made a discovery as we were scraping paint in the upper hall. The lovely old banisters stopped abruptly when you reached hall level and from there, until you came to the little door dividing the two parts of the house, the place where the banister had been cased with painted plywood. I was up on a ladder when Maurice began to hack on it with a claw hammer, and in about fifteen minutes, he had pulled the casing free to reveal the remaining intact Victorian banisters. We sat on the floor amid the dust, the wreckage and the cobwebs and we cheered.

'I just *thought* that's how it would be,' said Maurice smugly. 'Why would the fellow who fixed up the flat make more work for himself by removing the banisters when he could just case them in? Look, give me five minutes. I'll be back to clear away all this. You take a break until I come back.'

I wondered had he no more cigarettes, or was he running away from the disturbed spiders which were spilling out of their dusty refuge and invading the hall. Maurice hated spiders but I didn't particularly mind them, except those of exceptional size. By the time he came back, I had swept the creatures up into a large paper bag for conveying later to the garden – the wretched plastic bag hadn't been invented then. Maurice looked greatly relieved as he flourished a wicker-clad bottle of Orvieto and two glasses in my direction.

'You agree this requires celebration?'

'I would agree about anything you thought required me to drink a glass of white Orvieto.'

'We sat down on the stairs after I had removed the grime from my hands and I was happy that his idea of a celebratory wine was the same as mine – those days champagne was out of the question except for weddings and christenings. I had first tasted this delectable stuff during my summer in Italy and so had he. We were in Italy at the same time but we were back in Dublin before we met. The Anno Santo had nothing to do with my visit, but it had with his because so many young people in Dublin took advantage of the special fares on offer to get to Rome. At least that was the plan, but on the way, as he curled up in his sleeping bag on the side of the road, his bike was stolen and so was all his money. He had to resist with difficulty killing all the friendly Italians, who looked with amusement at his blistered feet, as he walked the rest of the way, from Milan to Rome, and asked him if he had seen their wonderful post-war Italian film, *The Bicycle Thief,* by Vittorio de Sica.

'Thanks for the spiders', he said suddenly, grinning down from his step of the stairs.

'You haven't had them yet. I'm serving them to you fried in butter with mushrooms for breakfast. Look, I've saved them up in that bag down there.'

'Then you can have my share too and sit down to a royal feast', he said. 'Listen, did I ever tell you about that sunny day when I leaned over the ancient bridge in the Ticino district?'

'Probably, but I'll listen again if you top up my glass.'

'Well, you know it rained nearly the whole time when I was cycling over the Alps in 1950? Well, it did, just as badly as in Kerry during August, and I knew this mustn't be unusual when I came down into one of those little villages and saw very small children on their way home from school *all* outfitted with little child-sized umbrellas. I reckoned that if people bought special little umbrellas for their kids, then rain up there when it wasn't snowing was probably normal. So I stepped on the pedals and got the hell out of there as fast as I could, and after most of a day's heavy going I was down into the Ticino district – sunshine and vineyards and people working in straw hats and sandals. I could have eaten a bullock, but this was only the middle of the first of four weeks and I was conserving cash whenever I could. So in a little shop in the first sunny village I came to, I bought a loaf of new bread and a chunk of the local cheese, plus a litre of milk and a handful of cherries.'

'Mercifully, no village wine?'

'Well, no. I had another six hours cycling before me at least, to the next hostel. Definitely no wine. But I leaned the bike against this humpbacked bridge covered in flowering creeper, and with gob full of bread and cheese I leaned over to look into the water – a full racing stream with its creepers trailing into it. I was warm. I was eating precisely what this little place had to offer. I was happy, damn it.'

'But since this is your story, it has to have a calamitous ending?'

'Depends on what you mean by a calamity. When I straightened up again for another mouthful of cheese, and when I studied the hand that was holding it, I saw that both were entirely covered in ants. Big biting ants that were already halfway to covering my arm. They had invaded the bread and turned it black. The shock made me drop the food and stumble back on the bike again. I rode like the hammers of hell until I couldn't feel the ants any more, and then when I did feel them again, I realised they were in under my shirt and shorts and socks – everywhere.

When next I saw that little stream, it had become a river, so I stopped and threw off every stitch of clothes and then threw myself into the river and swam until I felt the brutes *had* to be drowned. I ended up by discarding every garment except my shorts which I washed in the river and put back on wet, and the cycling shoes, which seemed to be ant-free.'

'And the moral of this tale is...?'

'Never assume that you've earned *anything*. Sunshine after pissing rain will either burn you to a cinder or breed ants to devour your food. Believe you have earned a modest feast after a famine, and you'll find the maggots or the ants have got there first. On the other hand if you have no expectations life may be pleasant enough.'

'Like now?'

'Like now.' He was smiling of course and I didn't believe he had no expectations. I ran my hands once more over the smooth handiwork of a carpenter who by then must have been dead for the best part of a century and I was extraordinarily happy that his work had lived on after him. When the entire staircase (in a remarkably short time once we got started) had been painted white and had its oak handrail waxed and polished to the texture of silk, we had the further pleasure of seeing every carved rail put to a specific use. The smallest child learned to navigate safely upstairs and downstairs by those same banisters. The last child likely to have done that in this house lived there some time between 1870 and 1904. There were no children since then, until the first of ours.

When you bought an old house in those days, you had to forego the seven years' remission of rates offered to new house buyers, and be prepared for the shock every winter storm might bring to the roof, and you also had to be prepared for the disapproval of most insurance companies. But when you bought an old house, you bought its history, you bought its trees, you bought the forsythia and the jasmine and the lilacs chosen by people long dead. You bought the spring bulbs those people had carried home in paper bags and planted with hope, and you bought, as in our case, the proliferation of self-renewal those bulbs provided every year. You bought the blackbirds and the thrushes which had been nesting for generations in the beech tree, and you bought the wrens which chose the hawthorn hedge that had meekly bent itself away from the prevailing winds. You bought the shards of broken pottery and china, which for some reason had accumulated under the raspberry bushes near the poplar tree at the end of the back garden. When the time came to renew the raspberry canes, you fingered the faded or still bright colours and tried to imagine the plates and the water jugs and the old soup toureens which had been set out for long-ago festivities.

Sometimes you bought the ghosts too. Ours was the benevolent cousin who was largely responsible for laying out the back garden. He had a passion for rockeries and unusual Alpine plants and sometimes – they were innocent days – he brought home a slip or a small root from his solitary walking tours in Wicklow but *only* (we were assured) from places where such plants were as plentiful as daisies. Maurice disapproved of such a habit, but I didn't. We called our gentle ghost Horatio, because we didn't remember his first name.

Sometimes Maurice would be out presenting a weekly programme, which he also edited, called *Plays of the Week*, from the old Radio Eireann studios in Henry Street. I would hear him letting himself in upstairs through the main hall, and walking across the as yet uncarpeted floor to the bathroom. This was our own bathroom when we had rented the apartment, but it had been made, together with our kitchen on the other side of the partition wall, from a tall-windowed back bedroom which used to be Mr Carroll's. Little fragile plants were, I believe, nurtured on the sunny granite windowsills and no doubt he watched for signs of growth each morning before he went out to work in the bank. Horatio's footsteps used to disappear into that room.

The fact that we had a ghost sharing the house with us didn't particularly bother us because he obviously meant us no harm. But I can't pretend it wasn't spooky occasionally, to look up from a book downstairs on hearing footsteps in the upper hall and go to the living room door to call hello. There would be no answering call from Maurice, because it wasn't Maurice. He would come in maybe fifteen minutes later (after a drink with the radio programme's producer in the Opal Bar) and would run downstairs straight away to relate the night's events.

There were no recorded programmes then: everything was live. And if some reviewer around the table had a cough, you heard it partly muffled by a handkerchief all through the programme. If Horatio had come in from a late mountain walk and gone straight into his own room, I would tell Maurice that, after he had finished his story. A rationalist in every other way, he believed in ghosts. In fact, he had once seen a ghost, at Moll Goggin's corner near the lighthouse in Youghal. He was a schoolboy then, down as usual with his grandparents on holiday, and with a few friends, he had been on his way for a swim out near Claycastle. A woman in a straggling long skirt approached them at the corner and, polite young fellow that he was, he stepped onto the roadway to let her pass.

'Why did you do that, Kennedy, with a car coming straight at you?' One of the friends asked.

'To let that old woman pass, of course.'

'What old woman?'

They all looked back. There was nobody on the pavement behind them. Maurice crossed to the other side of the road to look back beyond the bend in the pavement, but there was nobody.

The friends were local fellows and quite blasé about the occurrence. 'It's only old Moll Goggin so,' one of them said. 'Some folk see her and some don't. The Da knows all about her. She used to wait to see her man coming in on the boats just there below at the market dock. One wild night he didn't come in with the rest, and she went on waiting for his boat to appear from this headland ever after, at the turn of the tide. Everybody

160

knew about her when the aul fella was at school, but I haven't heard tell of her for a long while.'

'She's no harm', another of the group said. 'She does no banshee wailing and she never says a word. Fellows just see her sometimes – you know her by the raggedy old clothes. It all happened, according to the uncle, about a hundred years ago in the autumn time of the year. October winds did for him, the uncle said. Swept him over, like, when he was pulling in the nets. Sharks likely got him, because they never found his body. That's why old Moll went on believing she'd see her man sailing in on the tide some fine day, good as new. She died astray in the head, they say.'

We had never heard any hint of why Horatio had elected not to stay in his grave, and it never bothered us. I thought it might be interesting to mention the footsteps to Miss Nisbet, but Maurice was so against the idea that I never did. He was probably right that it would upset and worry her. And he was probably also right when he said Miss Nisbet had probably not seen or heard of Horatio.

Oddly enough, none of the children mentioned hearing anything, although our daughter's room was down three or four steps from the upper hall. Maurice had another of his theories about why Horatio had reactivated himself after we had bought the house. Maev was eight or nine at this time, no longer a baby. Poltergeists, for instance, can be recalled into activity by pre-adolescent girls, but poltergeists, as I pointed out, are troublesome, noisy and impossible to ignore. Horatio was a quiet soul, as befitted a man who spent most of his time tramping the Wicklow hills in search of unusual plants. Why should he want to harm us?

So we absorbed Horatio, as we also came to terms with the strange but normal night-time sounds of an old house, the noisy lead pipes which dated, like the house, from 1870, the creaking shutters which were always drawn on stormy nights, the three sighing steps in the middle of the stairs which led to the lower hall, the actual settling of the house into sleep, like the occupants, when the daytime sounds had died away. This was when you heard the breathing of the Beech tree, like small breaking waves, heard through open windows on warm breezy nights. There was this feeling that we had, so to speak, bought them all with the house, that they absorbed us as benevolently as we did them.

But once while we were all away on holiday, there was a strange story awaiting our return. Ronán Conroy was one of the school friends who loved cats and who volunteered to come in every day we were away to feed ours. He had fallen asleep in his friend Maev's room one warm evening with the cat curled beside him on the bed. He wakened up some hours later feeling chilled and scared – darkness outside, no cat and the sound of footsteps coming across the hall which was four steps above him. He jumped up and out onto the landing which was colder still. No sign of the cat. No sight of an intruder. No sound now of the footsteps, just this illogical cold as though he were inside a cloud near the top of a mountain – he like ourselves was a frequent hill walker. It took no time at all for Ronán to make up his mind. He quickly checked the bathroom into which the footsteps had faded. Nobody. He checked the spare bedroom beside it. Nobody.

'And then', said Ronán, 'I did what any man worth his salt would do. I ran like hell out of the freezing cold house and into the warm air outside. But, before you ask me, I *did* go back the next day and every day to feed the cat. Why should she suffer? But I took care never to fall asleep again.'

We didn't know what to make of this story, and at this stage I don't know whether or not Ronán knew about Horatio and embroidered this bad dream around him. But I do remember that my confidence in the benevolence of our ghost didn't alter. We decided, Maurice and I, that one of two things had happened: that Ronán had had a bad semi-waking dream sparked by what he had heard about Horatio; or alternatively Ronán's presence, his highly original and sceptical personality, had disturbed Horatio and caused that hostile atmosphere. It never happened again, but eventually Horatio seems to have melted into eternity on one of his own mountain walks. We simply stopped hearing him. Did this happen when the last of the children had moved out? I can't remember. But I don't think I sold that ghost with the house, when eventually I was living alone there, with too much empty space all around me. Horatio was in every sense of the word *our* ghost. I think he began and ended with *us*, maybe because we loved so much the garden he had planted.

The case of Dom Bowe, the genius stage carpenter of the Gate Theatre, is I think fairly similar. As I mentioned earlier, the story was told to me by Mícheál Mac Liammóir a few years before his death. It was obvious that the character and fidelity of Dom Bowe still haunted him, and that remorse played some part in it. I shall relate the story as closely as I can in Mícheál's own words:

Dom Bowe wasn't just a divine stage carpenter who knew exactly what you wanted when you showed him a few hasty squiggles on the back of an envelope. He was an artist and a marvellous worker and he could make anything. You could take away a table he had made as a prop for instance, and use it for years afterwards in the kitchen if you wanted to. He worked every hour God sent and we couldn't afford to pay him properly – of course we couldn't. We were all dirt poor then. One winter he got sick with pneumonia and he wouldn't stay in bed as long as he should have done. He came back to work in the draughty scene dock and one night when everybody had gone home after the show, he killed himself by walking through an upper window. A week later I was the last to leave the theatre and, as I was locking up, I heard the sound of somebody sawing wood and then in a few minutes I heard loud hammering. Immediately I

163

thought of Dom Bowe, but of course he was dead. When I went back to search the scene dock, there was nobody. As I was leaving for the second time, I heard the sawing again and I went back and unkindly wakened up a sort of caretaker who lived in a flat at the top of the theatre, but she had heard nothing.

Then a few days later when I was coming in to rehearsal, Dom's mother accosted me on the stairs and made a terrible scene. She said we should sell the cursèd theatre which had killed her son. He had slaved for us she said (which was perfectly true), always sawing up wood and making sets after hours while we went to wild parties and had a sinfully good time. I told her we mostly went home to cook up something cheap and simple and learn our lines for the next show before going to bed, but she raved on. I don't know what happened to her eventually.

A few years after, Hilton was coming down South Anne Street when he met Dom Bowe at the corner. Dom called out, 'Hello Hilton - how's Micheál?', and walked a few steps chatting with him to Burton's window. But when Hilton for some reason looked into that window he only saw his own face pale and shrinking because the man he had seen and spoken to was already dead – several years dead. Maybe dear Dom Bowe is still walking around Dublin but of course nobody would recognise him now, would they? Hilton and I don't walk around much any more, so we can't say if Dom's ghost still does.'

I think myself that ghosts are probably as thick as green leaves in April but we mostly don't see them. I think it is obvious too that there are bad ghosts and good ghosts. Knowing that a good ghost is around somewhere just out of sight in one's house has never bothered me. But when we were house-hunting at the end of the nineteen fifties, we once or twice sensed the other sort, notably one summer's afternoon in Kenilworth Square, Rathgar. It was a large mid-Victorian house with a square porch and it was newly decorated, an unusual thing at the time. Peadar O'Donnell said we should buy a bigger house than we needed, and turn half of it into an income instead of a liability. That would be the smart thing to do, Peadar said, one day when I ran into him in town.

The sun shone with unusual ferocity the day we got the key from the auctioneer. When we let ourselves in, yellow light streamed down the staircase from a tall round-headed window on the landing which had a border of deep blue glass. Almost immediately, Maurice said he would like to take a look first at the garden and I should wander around and see how the house pleased me. He vanished down a small flight of stairs towards the kitchen quarters, and I stood for a minute savouring the sunshine before pushing open the door on the left which led to two large interconnecting reception rooms. It was as though some weight on the other side of the door were pushing against my weight. I took only a quick glance at the beautifully moulded ceilings before moving towards the staircase and the golden light from the window.

Then I walked halfway up stairs wondering why there seemed to be light but no heat from the sun. The decision to join Maurice in the garden took me by surprise, but I followed him anyhow and found a small country style back door at the bottom of the steps leading to the garden, which, beyond the concrete yard, was huge and overgrown. I followed a briary path under a pergola and found Maurice among the tall meadow-grasses, standing with his hands in his pockets staring back at the house. Although we had seen sunshine on the staircase, the whole house was now in deep shadow and somehow menacing.

'What do you think? James Joyce was born just over there', I said. 'It's priced away below the going rate.'

'I don't care if they're giving it away', Maurice said. 'Let's get the hell out of here.' He grabbed my hand and we literally ran back through the side door and into the house. What I'll never understand is that I wasn't even tempted to take a backward look at the huge old kitchen, usually the place I would have examined first. We dashed up the steps and along the hall and Maurice pushed me out first before coming through himself and slamming the heavy oak door behind us. It felt like an escape from some unknown evil. We were both breathless and not inclined to talk about it. It was several years before we learned by accident that nobody had ever stayed in ownership of that house for longer than a couple of months. It was said to be haunted by a murdered wife, and one of its nastier tricks was lighting itself up like an ocean liner when nobody was inside, and switching itself off before anybody put a key in the door (this, of course, was two decades before self-activating security lights). What I wondered was why anybody had ever decided to buy it in the first place since we had caught danger signals from our first entry.

Ironically, however, it was one of our own grown children, Conor, who innocently tied himself into renting for two years a bijou country residence with a river flowing by its hall door and a spectacular shell-room which ensured that nobody could ever sleep a peaceful night in that house. Haunted? It was positively polluted by malevolence, although no sound of any sort was ever heard. Verily, if your mind misdoubt you aught, obey it.

In 1969, ghosts of a different sort began to rise up and challenge us. That was some time after the civil rights marches in the North and the horrific events at Burntollet and what became known as the Battle of the Bogside. The Taoiseach Jack Lynch made his most famous speech, a few sentences of which were read over the phone to me by a friend whom I never would have guessed had Republican sympathies. I had been out for a hike and hadn't heard the news bulletin. The few sentences I heard over the phone were: 'The present situation is the inevitable outcome of policies pursued for decades by successive Stormont governments. It is clear also that the Irish government can no longer stand by and see innocent people injured and perhaps worse.' He goes on about the RUC no longer being recognised as an impartial force by the Roman Catholics and ends up calling for urgent talks with the British government because – and I'm quoting again: 'Reunification of the national territory can provide the only permanent solution to the problem."

There was an element of excitement in the friend's voice that was not echoed by Maurice when I told him, 'So it's time to take out the shotguns and the rosary beads from the thatch again, is it?'

Prime Minister Harold Wilson clearly took a more serious view and after his visit to the Home Office, when he wrote in his journal: 'We had to consider the possibility that within the next 24 hours we might face Civil War in the North and an invasion from the South.'

Throughout the previous summer the television screens had been crowded with rioting Roman Catholics and marching Ulster Protestants, with pitched battles in the streets and petrol bombs lobbed by jeering teenagers into the police lines. What looked like Civil War in microcosm had become a commonplace of the news bulletins by the autumn of that year, but this announcement was still startling. For me it brought back a childhood image of myself sitting at home on the kitchen table swinging my legs and listening to the faltering voice of Neville Chamberlain announcing that from that moment Great Britain was at war with Germany. It was 3 of September 1939, a damp and misty Sunday morning and I was about fourteen. 'War' in the abstract had an exciting ring of times past about it, of military bands and polished brass buttons, of laughing soldiers leaning out of railway carriages and waving goodbye to clusters of girls in cotton dresses at little country railway stations. It was the stuff of Hollywood movies and faded newspaper cuttings in old albums – my godmother had kept one. I remember thinking that school couldn't possibly be so boring now that a war was on. We had been fired quite recently by Thackeray's account of the night before the Battle of Waterloo. Once my father had read to us Charles Wolfe's 'The Burial of Sir John Moore After Corunna,' and the tears flowed long before the end of it but also the pulses raced faster.

The reality in Eamon de Valera's Ireland was different: neutrality, food rationing and gas masks carefully stored away in the bottom drawer of the wardrobe. On the credit side there were occasional parcels of food, chocolate and oranges from my father's friends in the North. And much later, when rumours of concentration camps and the torture of Jews, even children, began slowly to trickle through, my father said it was Churchill's insidious propaganda, and couldn't possibly be true.

All that had been long ago, and now there might be war again within our own shores, Civil War, which old people said was the worst kind of war. And my own children too, when we finally bought a television set in the mid-sixties, had sat around watching the highly dramatic and emotive programmes, wonderfully scripted by Hugh Leonard, which RTE put on to commemorate the 50th anniversary of the Easter Rising. I remember fetching out their grandfather's old medals and notebooks, the book of parodies he wrote, his book from Ballykinler camp and the sepia photographs of laughing young men in Camp No. 2. *An Tine Beó*? (The Living Fire) Yes, but it seemed to me that it would have been a betrayal if I had *not* brought my Republican parents into the picture. Maurice quietly disapproved, and he was proved to be right. How many children in Northern Ireland had similarly been brainwashed and developed into stone-throwing young thugs who progressed to throwing petrol bombs into 'enemy' forces in their district, and from there into the raw recruits of the revitalised IRA. 'Tiocfaidh ár lá' (Our Day Will Come) appeared scrawled on surfaces everywhere, north and south.

It was some time in the late nineteen seventies that I realised from first-hand experience just quite how brainwashed young children could be, and it chilled me. Under the Arts Council Writers in Schools project, I was visiting a couple of schools in Derry, one of them Roman Catholic School in the Bogside. I discussed with them Frank O'Connor's wonderful story Guests of the Nation, that dramatic and searing tale of the British captives Belcher and Hawkins who become the best of friends with the IRA unit holding them in a remote farmhouse in the heart of West Cork. They all play cards together every night, and during the daytime help the old woman with household chores. Suddenly word comes down from the Revolutionary Council that several Irish hostages may be executed and if so, Belcher and Hawkins must be dispatched too. Young members of the unit remind their commanding officer that they have all become friends – haven't the local girls taught them all to dance 'The Siege of Ennis' and 'The Walls of Limerick'? The two Englishmen are similarly incredulous. Haven't they all become good chums together? When the order comes down from on high, Commanding Officer Donovan even rejects Hawkins' offer to fight alongside his Irish comrades if they will only give him a gun. Hawkins and the amiable Belcher are summarily marched down to the bog and shot dead. The story ends with the old woman of the house going down on her knees to pray for the souls of the Tommies, and with this bleak passage from the man who had to shoot them:

> ... with me it was ... as though the patch of bog where the two Englishmen were was a thousand miles away from me, and even Noble, mumbling just behind me, and the old woman and the birds and the bloody stars were all far away, and I was somehow very small and very lonely. And anything that happened ever me after, I never felt the same about again.

The two questions I asked the Bogside children were: Was the commanding officer right to order the execution of Belcher and Hawkins? And were his men right to carry out his order? There was a brief silence as the children smiled knowingly around at one another, and then pityingly at me. Their verdict was unanimous as one voice after another spoke up.

'The officer *was* right, Miss, to give the order. Those so-called soldiers were Brits fighting a war with *us* in *our* country.'

'An' if the men hadna obeyed they'd never be able to lift their heads again, would they, Miss?'

'An', howsomever theyda been shot themselves.'

'Their lives wouldna been worth a stick of toffee, would they?'

'But', I said, 'don't you think at least that the IRA men who were ordered to shoot down their two friends were being asked to do something very brutal? Very difficult? Those men had *become* their friends.

Heads were shaken and shoulders shrugged all around me. Two more voices were lifted.

'You can't be friends with the enemy, Miss. Two at least of *us* were shot down like dogs by *them*, weren't they? That's why Belcher and Hawkins had to be shot.'

'It was only *fair*, wasn't it?'

'But, you see, I think that Frank O'Connor wasn't just telling a good story. I think he was trying to show us what a terrible thing war is, and what terrible things it makes people do to one another individually, even after they have *become* friends.'

These children of twelve and thirteen were no longer interested. The poor pale and deprived faces expressed no conflict either. They were so sure they were right. These children could remember no other background to their lives but petrol bombs, rubber bullets and street fighting and the 'vanished' fathers of their friends who had been 'lifted'. I found it all profoundly depressing.

Later, outside in their street, I walked down the steep slope to the river Foyle in windy sunshine, glad that I was going to have lunch in cheerful company. I saw that I had, in fact, entered *Free Derry*, as the wall slogans said. It was two weeks before Easter and there was a splurge of tulips and daffodils in the tiny gardens. On the gable ends of the neat terraced houses were painted flowers, mostly tall white lilies flanking the coffins that were decorated with black berets and tricolours. 'Tiocfaidh ár lá', the captions said.

One excellently painted gable end reminded me of a sketch one of my father's fellow prisoners in Ballykinlar Camp had put into his album after the rising of 1916. That same image was used as a logo by a Dublin firm which manufactured stationery during the nineteen twenties and thirties: a round tower with a sunburst behind it and, at its base, the goddess Banba, with her flowing hair, her harp and her faithful hound at her feet. In Derry there was an addition, 'Tiocfaidh ár lá', it said.

I stood at one corner of the Diamond a while later and waited for the enemy to pass by. They were sitting on what looked like old-fashioned school benches on both sides of an open-backed army lorry, waiting for the traffic lights to change. The last in line was nearest to me as I waited. He was about eighteen years old and was cradling in his arms, and stroking with one finger, a very small puppy which had sore eyes. I was glad that I was on my way to see the irrepressible Seán McMahon and (I think) Michael O'Donnell the bookseller, whose beautiful little shop then stood in a street of ruins, the once elegant Shipquay Street.

Another street I knew well in Ben Kiely's Omagh, was blasted into incinerated fragments, together with the young and the old, the born and the unborn who just happened to be there on a sunny Saturday in August, the 15th of August to be exact, the birthday of that same author of *Proxopera*. This was twenty years after I saw one of the enemy cradling his puppy in Derry, and it was many hundreds of bombings and murders and beatings and cripplings later, at a time when hopes had been raised by the IRA ceasefire – a ceasefire rejected by this particular fundamentalist faction. Truly, we had fed the heart on fantasies and the heart had grown brutal on the fare. Despite the renewed clamour for decommissioning which this outrage provoked, many months after the Omagh bombing the dogs of war were still crouched slavering over their weapons, having signed the 1998 Good Friday Agreement a year earlier, and having failed to deliver as much as an ounce of semtex as a gesture of peace.

Some years earlier in 1979, we had been at a party in Dublin the day Earl Mountbatton was blown to atoms in his yacht, together with two young boys. Mountbattan's mother-in-law was injured, but recovered. The cut-off point at the party we attended that night was 10.00 pm, but on our way out we were beckoned hospitably into an inner sanctum walled with books. The select company in there included a well-known barrister, a couple of writers, a few politicians, a financier, an editor and some superb musicians. To the strains of 'Oro, sé do bhaithe abhaile' the bottles of *Veuve Clicquot* were being cracked open to celebrate the Famous Victory of Mountbatton's murder. We were shocked beyond speech, and got out of the room faster than we had gone in.

Then one night in the Tyrone Guthrie Centre at Annamackerrig a journalist rose up in arms to defend what she termed the concept of 'legitimate targets' in the North. It was a time when the Loyalist terror had temporarily died down, but the IRA of several varieties were nightly launching attacks on individual members of 'the army of occupation' as they called it, and at the same time maiming, shooting dead, kidnapping or 'disappearing' members of their own community who dared to disagree with them. The most brutal and infamous of these terrible atrocities was the abduction of Mrs Jean McConville in 1972, torn away from her family of young children in Belfast because she went down to her front gate with a drink of water for a dying young British soldier. It took all of twenty years for

172

the IRA to admit to murdering her, and to assist in finding her body eventually, on a beach in County Louth in August, 2003.

To get back to the journalist, however. She was loud in voicing the old arguments: that what we needed was not less but more violence in the cause of a united Ireland and ultimate peace. The irony is that the IRA's major electoral advances have always been at times when people believed they were moving away from rather than towards the gun.

Comparisons were inevitable with what I remembered from stories told in my childhood of revolutionary Ireland's glory days – romantic stories of men on the run, fondly cared for by lovely young women in remote parts of Ireland and in cities too. They cropped up in conversation as inevitably as other Dublin gossip. *Safe* houses were remembered with respect, my grandmother's among them. Many of these houses had proudly displayed on the parlour wall a well-worked macramé bag made by a prisoner in Frongoch or Ballykinlar camps. Many of them displayed emblems like a harp or a cluster of shamrock carved from meatbones. In my grandmother's house there were old Abbey Theatre playbills – black on sulphur yellow – of productions mounted by my father after the release of the IRA volunteers in December, 1916. One of the playbills, which hangs on my own wall at the moment, trumpets the announcement: 'First performance outside barbed wire, The Ballykinlar Players (founded by the Rajah of Frongoch) in *The Lord Mayor* by Edward McNulty.'

My father, that same Rajah, was also among the cast. The whole feeling of those post-revolutionary days is very well caught by Julia O'Faoláin in a short story she called, *A Bunch of Sweet Herbs*. The schoolgirl narrator believes sadly that romantic Ireland is indeed dead and gone - it died with the youth of her romantic revolutionary parents.

Seán O'Faoláin seems to endorse this in his preface to his first collection of short stories, *A Midsummer Night's Madness*: 'I had come out of an experience that left me dazed, the revolutionary period in Ireland. Not that it was really an experience as I now understand the word. It was too filled with dreams and ideals and a sense of dedication to be an experience in the meaning of things perceived, understood and remembered.'

But remembered in the national consciousness the glory days were. Romantic Ireland was not really dead and gone, as Yeats believed. It was waiting like covered embers to be blown into life again in the nineteen sixties by a number of things. The rise, for instance, of a new generation of educated young people in the North who were no longer content to be second-class citizens under Unionist rule. It is ironic that the opening in the mid-nineteen sixties of Queen's University, under Terence O'Neill, to the Roman Catholic working-class youth, was indirectly responsible for the Civil Rights marches and the exuberant outburst of civil disobedience that ultimately led to infiltration by the IRA and a state of tension close to Civil War. Paisley and others eagerly fanned the flames and I truly believe that the 50th Anniversary of the 1916 Rising did the rest.

There was, of course, a rising tide of student unrest throughout Europe and in the United States too. In 1968, *Les Evenements* happened in Paris and the young of the United States started to march with Martin Luther King and against the Vietnam war. We were already, because of television, becoming a small world, with revolutionary influences coming in from everywhere.

However, I remember long ago, when only a crackling 'wireless' in the corner connected us to the outside world, being overcome with disgust during a history lesson in school to learn that Daniel O'Connell, 'The Liberator', believed that the freeing of Ireland from English rule was not worth a single drop of Irish blood. That was reputedly because he witnessed post-revolutionary bloodshed in Paris, but the French Revolution and its excesses, on the other hand, had inspired other Irishmen like Robert Emmet and Wolfe Tone. The 1798

Rebellion was the result, and after it, the Fenian uprising, which through John O'Leary directly influenced the 1916 Rising. The line was unbroken right up to the 'Troubles' in the North. An Tine Beo? When the conditions were finally ripe for a solution, key individuals were not prepared to let go of their grudges.

During the summer of 1970 we left the television screens behind and thankfully took a carful of children to the south of France, to Montpellier. I had been for a couple of years writing a television column for the *Evening Press* and, with the blessing of my editor, Conor O'Brien (who used to say he was not Conor News O'Brien nor Conor Cruise O'Brien but Conor *The* O'Brien) I left my column in the good care of my old friend Joe Reynolds, and happily escaped to the sun.

For a few summers before this we had exchanged our daughter for five or six weeks with a French girl from Montpellier, who took with instant approval to life in Dublin. Laure Calvet – soon to be replaced by her sister Lise and her brother Georgie – had given Ireland such a good press that her parents decided they must come too to see what all the fuss was about, so we planned to exchange houses for a month or so. It was the year after General de Gaulle had visited Ireland and an influx of French visitors to Ireland began. They became nearly as numerous on the streets as the Americans.

In truth, as we coped with the expenses of maintaining a biggish house and three children at school, we had taken only Irish holidays for many years, and this French journey was a particular delight for us – the smells of good coffee and garlic and Gauloises again, the sun, the challenge of it. Our car wasn't really a tourer but a grey second-hand Morris 11, the newest and the most elegant of all the old cars we had owned. This one I remember with particular affection because I had made enough money from journalism to share equally the cost of buying it with Maurice, and I had chosen it a couple of years previously. To prepare it for the marathon drive south from Le Havre, he had fitted it with several costly additions, but one thing had not been thought of, and that was the fact that Irish headlights dip towards the left and we were now driving on the right. So all through the hot dark night we were flashed at angrily by an unending stream of lorry drivers going north, and sometimes we were hooted at as well. Bloody tourists! The boys, when they wakened up, thought it superb fun, but it was a driving nightmare. Sometimes the lorry drivers came so close that I feared we would be squashed, and end up as just an added collection of flies on their windscreens. It was worse *not* to be driving, I think, but Maurice had taught me to drive, and never henceforth would consent to be driven, with me at the wheel. Very wise, I'm sure, since he had to endure a lot in the course of introducing a mechanical illiterate like me to locomotion. Eventually, at my suggestion, we decided to put up at a country inn, called Les Chausseurs, which, because it was so late, could feed us only superb cheese, bread and local red wine for supper.

The next morning, out walking around before anybody else was awake, I discovered a beautiful old barn with a clotheslines hanging from its cross beams and snow white cotton sheets billowing like sails in the crisp breeze. And in the drive I found a large grey Renault decked out for a wedding, with bows of tulle tied on all the doors and more tulle threaded through with white carnations strung across the dashboard. Somehow this cheerful sight, and the billowing white sails of the sheets seemed like a good omen. Maybe this would be a very good holiday.

Provence glimpsed from the autoroute that day was the dream one had dreamed long ago on seeing the first Van Gogh – burnt Sienna brick in the shuttered houses, little cypresses, young poplars on the skyline, snow on the faraway Savoy Alps, blinding amber sunlight, terraced fields. The river at Lyon was broad and beautiful.

We were to stay in the lovely Montpellier house of Gérard and Yvonne Calvet, which had Gerard's paintings covering every wall and a beautiful garden where I would write in the mornings during our stay. After a *trés simple* lunch on our arrival – which was in fact elaborate and delicious – there was coffee and *fine champagne* under a sunshade on the terrace. We were shown Gérard's two ateliers, where he worked hard both after and before his swimming and sailing – my idea of the perfect life! Later in the month, I bought an oil painting and a large charcol drawing by our host which still today hold pride of place in my study, and now on the cover of this book.

Whenever the children were happily occupied and supervised and Maurice was reading *Paris Match* or *Le Sud*, to which he became addicted, I just wandered and watched. There was an element of eternity about the old men in straw hats playing Boules in open squares under the trees, or in the shade of Les Arceaux, which date from Roman times.

In smaller towns, and even in the old parts of Montpellier, women sat in groups on the pavement outside old houses and sewed while watching the world go by. Like old Youghal women in The Mall. Like many of the Vermeer women.

During our stay introductions through the Calvets' extraordinary network of friends opened the doors of chateaux and castles which had survived the Revolution in dilapidated splendour. We walked the baking streets of towns whose names were so familiar from paintings and novels, and danced, of course, on the Pont d'Avignon.

We visited the extraordinary medieval village of St Guilhem le Désert, which seemed to me without equal anywhere I'd seen. There was no trace of this past or the previous century anywhere. Only steep narrow streets no wider than an arms-length and ancient stone steps leading to bronze tongued fountains. Inside a church by the square, it was as cool as a tomb under the stone arches, and nearby women had left wine for the evening meal to cool in gushing waters, on stone the colour of old honey. A few spoiled cats stalked around.

We visited Arles, with its pavement cafés, like Van Gogh's night café and from a balcony looked out over the red rooftops beloved of Vincent. Beyond, the broad blue Rhône shimmered in the heat. It was a holiday of white hot days, with very little wind, rambles in the country, irresistible rural inns with tables set out under trees, and mile after mile of burning landscapes, including the *Chateauneuf-du-Pape* vineyards without a single inn or restaurant in sight.

July moved along and it was too short a time before the days of wine and ice-cold pastis would draw to a close for us, and one morning neither Maev nor I went swimming. Instead, we did everybody's washing – the last task of all holidays, all love affairs with idle summer days, when routines are not even remembered, much less followed.

After a farewell dinner with the Calvet family, we set off early drove up through France on a punishing drive just in time to catch the ferry at La Havre. The following morning the sky above deck of our ship bound for home was grey and cool, with some hazy sun trying to break through. Home? Even our own house would seem strange to us when we saw it again. Not to speak of our dark and rainy town, where, when the bank strike was over, we would learn the true state of our finances. Yet as I poured fresh breakfast coffee for Maurice, I watched his grin slowly appearing with the new plate of croissants, which the waiter placed at his elbow. We'd had the holiday of a lifetime. *Courage, mon ami, le diable est mort!*

12

Years like Great Black Oxen

Where did they go, the rest of those years between 1959 when Myles Kennedy was born and 1992 when his father died? I had never ceased to push the pen along, as Seán Ó'Faoláin used to say but with the problems and delights of family life there never seemed to be a time when one could work steadily on a long-term project. I certainly wrote and published some short stories here and there, I was a regular broadcaster on Irish radio and I did a fortnightly piece on new fiction for Jack White of *The Irish Times*. Through this, I encountered the *nouveau roman* of the sixties – Robbe-Grillet, Nathalie Sarraute, Marguerite Duras and the great Beckett, who gave stature to the movement.

There was matter for a thesis (and probably hundreds of them were written) on what made Beckett different from the rest; why the lack of a conventional structure made him uniquely interesting and those dozens of others merely showy and trendy and ultimately dull – to me at any rate. It wasn't that I wasn't young enough to welcome difference, but having carefully weighed it, I honestly found it lacking. If a novel can't drive a reader forward under its own momentum, as, say, *Ulysses* can and *À la Recherche du Temps Perdus* and *At Swim-Two-Birds*, then you have a very good reason why new writers of the fifties and sixties are practically unread today and largely forgotten. I realised this not so long ago when I was weeding out my own shelves and Michael, a very good bookseller in my adopted village, handed a dozen or more new novels in pristine condition back to me and said, 'Unfortunately we can't take these. They were well reviewed but they didn't sell very well in the 'sixties – and they don't sell at all now.'

Two novels of that period stand out, however, in my mind, the first being William Trevor's *The Old Boys* and the other *Albert Angelo* by B. S. Johnson, an English poet just beginning to be recognised, who had launched out suddenly into wonderful fiction. I was lucky that both came my way from the *Irish Times* and the surreal element in both was by way of an exciting shock to the imagination. Both answered the question: apart from a useful cheque now and again, why am I doing this?

The fame of William Trevor burns brighter with every new book, but the name of Bryan Johnson causes few flickers of recognition even among bookmen.

B. S. Johnson died by his own hand when he was almost forty, just a few years after he had phoned me one evening in Dublin and come to supper, bearing on one arm his wife Virginia and under the other a particularly fine salmon that he had caught that morning in the River Moy. Virginia was extremely attractive and excellent company, while he was silent and shy, a big Englishman whose world had radically changed since he had first read Joyce at the age of twenty. London born, but with Irish blood on one side of his family, he had responded with several long lyrical pages to my review, presumably because I had commented on the strong Joycean rhythms of his prose. I next encountered his work about five years later when I was writing a weekly television column for the *Evening Press*.

I reviewed one of the oddest BBC offerings ever to appear at that time on the small screen, a documentary called *Fat Man on a Beach*, written and presented by B. S. Johnson

was for Dublin were ignored. Hardly anybody with power would listen, and some of those who abused their power did so for the most venal and contemptible of reasons, the details of which were murkily emerging only in the late nineteen nineties. It has provided a few hollow laughs for me and my kind that sometimes the demolition of the very worst monstrosities is not necessary; they fall down piece by piece themselves, like the government buildings adjacent to the Shelbourne, for instance, and the Canadian Embassy. Sometimes they are rebuilt at enormous expense to the taxpayer, probably only to stay serviceable for a further twenty-five or thirty years. Longevity is the only virtue that can be claimed by Desmond FitzGerald's O'Connell Bridge House, by the way, one of the first and worst of these repellent buildings, which unfortunately does not fall down. It is truly sad to reflect that Dublin was precipitated into ruin not by poverty and neglect but largely by the boom-time of the sixties when developers like Matt, and later Patrick, Gallagher bulldozed their way unhindered though our heritage.

Looking back – and I can clearly remember the physical Dublin of seventy years ago – it is the actual fabric of the streets I remember and the clang of electric trams, and newly plopped horsedung steaming in the sun but smelling only of wet grass, and newsboys singing out 'Heggle-aw-Mayel?' (Herald or Mail?) and the huge elephant above the entrance to Elvery's in O'Connell Street which you could see best from the open top of a tram, and going into the zoo under the little thatched house that marked the entrance, and the old graveyard in Drumcondra with which I opened this book. They are all more immediate to me now than any new building – even the one or two good ones.

Years passed, as the Victorian female novelists were fond of noting, and so, despite the depredations without, they did too for me within. As I have mentioned, I worked seriously for a number of years on a book called *Antiquities*, recasting it several times and then radically revising it. I'd always tried to remember O'Faoláin's dictum 'Revision is part of the art of writing', and there were times over those years when it was positively enjoyable to be a savage censor because I knew the loamy stuff that went into that book was worth it, even before I got a verifying letter from Sean himself. It was quite difficult to let it leave my hands but when at last I did, my agent Pat Kavanagh sold it quickly to André Deutsch in London and it was published in the spring of 1978, with a reception for a hundred people in the newly restored Tailors' Hall.

This was useful because my previous book had appeared all of twenty-four years previously, and since then I had written nothing but journalism, a couple of children's books and the odd short story. The favourable reception of *Antiquities* sparked me into activity again and several novels followed. Then one morning I opened a letter from the Mayo County Librarian, Pat McMahon, asking if I would consider going to Castlebar as the county's first ever Writer-in-Residence. The appointment was to be for four months which could be divided into two semesters or as I wished. Some papers were included giving details of salary and conditions and he said he would like to meet me for lunch in Dublin to discuss the project. One sentence in his letter comes back to me: 'I hope this time in Mayo will be an enriching time for you as a writer.' He hadn't got money in mind and neither had I when I set off in a ten-year-old Austin Mini for what seemed to me a huge adventure, even more appealing, ultimately, than a similar North American trip the previous year. The only worry I had was about Maurice, whose health was steadily worsening. But he urged me to go, and two of the grown children who still lived at home did likewise. They would look after him, they promised, and I knew they were to be trusted.

Ever since the age of twenty when I first cycled across the new bridge at Achill, even earlier when I had come upon the Synge journals for the first time, the West of Ireland, the very mention of it, had always caused a quickening of the pulses. Somewhere far back an ancestor of mine had waved goodbye to his family in Connemara and gone, not west, as most of them had done, but east to Dublin. There are various versions of the name Mulkerns, but none of them except ours is to be encountered in Dublin. The first time I went to the Aran Islands (in 1948) I was graciously received as a kinswoman called *Ni Mhaolchiaráin*.

My reception in Castlebar was warmth itself. It was mid-November, bleak and blustery and almost dark by the time I arrived on an arranged corner of The Mall opposite the Imperial Hotel, where George Moore used to stay, and where the first meeting of the Land League took place. There indeed were Pat McMahon, his wife Kathleen and their little daughter Úna. I knew right from the start that these welcoming people were the sort I hoped to find. Kathleen was happily and hugely pregnant and remarked that (who knows?) it might just be tonight. She used to work in the Library of RTE and there was some chat and news exchanged about mutual friends. Pat was anxious about the lodgings he had found for me on a temporary basis. He mentioned a few cottages I might like to rent in the spring, one a converted schoolhouse on the edge of a lake. The atmosphere buzzed with euphoria, and the exquisite child in the red jumper smiled across the table and then watched me steadily with her enormous dark eyes. Remembering the problems of sibling rivalry, I silently hoped the new baby would not turn her little world abruptly upside down into anxiety and tears. We finished our wine, and emerged into the rainy darkness where I followed their car up the Westport Road to the home (called *Tonelegee*), of Phil and Ralph Jones.

As it happened, the Jones's and I became very good friends but that first wet night was not the most auspicious of beginnings. The house seemed cold after the big fires of the Imperial Hotel, but the welcome of Ralph Jones, a retired bank official, was warm. Mrs Jones was spending the evening with friends and Ralph prepared a lovely meal which he served to me in style. The family dog, a black poodle called Darkie, yapped furiously whenever he could escape from the kitchen and after the meal I decided to ingratiate myself with him by offering him a walk in the rain. He accepted graciously enough, Ralph thought it a good idea, and off we went into the suburbia which had not existed when I had last cycled through Castlebar on my way to Westport, a long time before.

Darkie was probably not used to rainy walks in the dark accompanied by strange females, and he made frenzied efforts to escape. The lead had no proper handle and it suddenly slipped through my cold fingers. The dog fled as though demons were at his tail, and I pursued but lost him – a black dog on a dark night. I searched for a while and then turned for home, believing he would most likely be there ahead of me. No. Mr Jones put on his tweed cap and politely tried to conceal his horror. I went out with him and we called, 'Darkie, Darkie'. Mr Jones mentioned that a dog no bigger than Darkie had been killed on this same road only a short while before – traffic to and from Westport was very heavy along the road. (The next morning I understood what he meant.) We went back in out of the rain, and Ralph said why not watch *The Late Late Show* with him – Darkie might come home by himself. I did not voice my fear that if he didn't, Mrs Jones most certainly could and probably would hand me straight over to the Guards. I didn't, however, meet Mrs Jones until the next day, but Darkie came back shivering and sodden after his adventure about two hours later. Occasionally when I gave up trying to dry and placate him, he would practically choke in his fury of barking at my ankles and then lift straight up off the carpet like a demented helicopter. Ralph locked him in the warm kitchen eventually and we returned to *The Late Late Show*. I suddenly remembered a childhood family holiday in Bray – it seems extraordinary, but Dublin families often did go all of the ten miles to Bray for their holidays. Anyhow we were staying in a guest house on that road of Victorian houses which runs from the town to the railway station, and one morning my brother Jim and I were allowed out alone to the beach on condition that we took good care of our baby brother Cyril, who was about four years old at the time. We forgot about him somewhere in the region of the Dodgems (which we called the Bumpers) and we spent the rest of that precious morning of 'freedom' looking for him. It rained and we went home, dispirited, to confess to our mother. Cyril was there before us, insufferably smug-looking and eating a hot buttered scone. He had, it seemed, found his own way home almost immediately and was discovered reaching up to knock at the door while shouting at the same time, 'They lost me! They lost me!' It seemed Darkie Jones felt the same way about me and wasn't going to let me forget it.

The following Monday was a day of introductions to the County Secretary, officially my employer, and to the library staff who were extremely friendly. There was a visit to an available flat I might like to rent: it was large and self-contained but decorated in such a lurid style that I knew it would drive me mad to live there, even with the inducement of slot-machine heating.

The nicest part of that day of flying wind and rain was when Pat handed me the keys of the book-walled office which would be mine for the duration of my stay. It was in the Old Linen Hall, now used as the Town Hall, a cut-stone eighteenth century building of some charm. Inside the locked door, it lost the somewhat neglected feeling of the entrance and became a luxurious study with a large mahogany table thoughtfully cleared and polished just for me. It had a phone and blocks of paper and the delight of all those bookshelves built into every wall and loaded with books, including reference books of every kind. Most were an overflow from the library which was already too small for an extremely book-conscious town and was approached by steep concrete steps which made access by wheelchair impossible, and very difficult, as the County Librarian pointed out, for elderly people with stiff joints. Already there was a gleam in Pat McMahon's eye which bespoke plans for a new library. In due course this materialised the year after I left Castlebar into a handsome building, beautifully designed and full of light and angled into a corner of the Mall, accessible and welcoming to young and old, able-bodied and handicapped alike, and always busy. His dream made flesh, Pat McMahon and his delightful family moved on, but that is jumping a few years ahead. I had a lot to learn and a fair amount to teach before I moved on myself. What remains with me to this day is a sense of kinship and several close ties with people who were all strangers to me up to the rainy moment when I drove into their lives.

Castlebar itself had anyhow remained locked warmly in my mind ever since I heard a fine actress, long dead, Bríd Ní Loinsigh, reading out her letter (the way people do who are unused to using a pen) even as she wrote it to Mr Seamus Mulroy, Wine and Spirit Dealer, Castlebar. I am in the Abbey Theatre with my parents at one of those matinees of the late thirties, and I have graduated to going with both of them to the theatre whenever something 'educational' is on offer. As a small child I sometimes went with my father, whenever my mother preferred to spend Saturday afternoon in some other way or if she had already seen the play. Now the rhythms of J. M. Synge are strange to my ear, but I got out of that theatre entrapped for life, totally at one with Synge's own enchantment. Yeats told him one day in Paris to go west and give a tongue to the sea-cliffs, and so he did, writing in the process one of the most magical love-scenes in Irish literature. That scene set my thirteen-year-old senses spinning, but from Pegeen's reading aloud from her letter in the very opening moments of *The Playboy* I was lost anyhow:

Six yards of stuff for to make a yellow gown. A pair of lace boots with lengthy heels on them and brassy eyes. A hat is suited for a wedding day. A fine-tooth comb. To be sent with three barrels of porter in Jimmy Farrell's creel cart on the evening of the coming fair to Mister Michael James Flaherty.

She sends it with the best compliments of the season, and she catches her lower lip between her teeth and silently reads the letter over again before licking the gum of the envelope and sealing it up.

I have seen the name Mulroy on one of the old painted shop fronts of Castlebar, and I am bewitched.

However unwelcoming the weather, I go for walks every morning before breakfast just to get the pure icy air into my lungs – it blows always in the same direction, south-east straight down from Nephin mountain. What if I *am* walking through villas whose architectural model is tourist Spain? I walk until they have petered out and I can hear a cock crowing into the cold air. I double back across the bog road where crows are already busy with their ungainly nests, where I know I shall hear the Cukoo calling in a few months' time. I come back to the barking of Darkie Jones – and I get my own breakfast in the quiet house. This is the time of course when I *ought* to be working on my own manuscript, but it doesn't happen because I know that the time for work is not open-ended and inevitably I would end up late at my office if I started to work properly. I don't like to feel rushed at something which is for me the best part of the day. Perhaps I can phrase this better. Working away with no sense of time and then realising that four hours have gone by is the best part of any day. But I'm lazy. I can find any number of good excuses why I would be better off working seriously in my office and not at a little card table in front of a window between two beds. The window shows me an expanse of green fields and a herd of cows beyond the garden wall. And beyond the cows I see a long low lime-washed farmhouse against the slopes of Nephin, with turf-smoke rising peacefully from the chimney.

As I've said, I did a lot of hard work during that spell in County Mayo (including the editing of *New Writing from the West*) but I did very little work of my own. I was too absorbed in the dynamic of the place. It took over. And sometimes I made breathtaking discoveries. For instance, one day in March when a Siberian gale was blowing outside the little library in Swinford, and I was listening to the handiwork of four hardy souls who had braved the weather because they thought I could teach them how to write. One of them, John Geraghty, asked a friend to read his manuscript. I listened with growing amazement and I could hardly believe what I was hearing, an updated but unmistakable version, in short story form, of Synge's play *In the Shadow of the Glen*. When it was finished, I could only respond with a joke, 'Are you sure your name is not John Millington Synge?'

The decent man didn't know what I was talking about, and he looked a little offended. He said his name was John Geraghty as anybody in Swinford could tell me. He had neither seen nor read Synge's play. He had heard the story from one of the visiting neighbours at his own house near Ballina, quite possibly in the same region where eighty years previously Synge himself heard that same story which he used as material for his play, although he set it in Wicklow. I was stunned. It's things like that which make poking around the West of Ireland as exciting today as ever it was when I was twenty-two and searching for traces of Synge in the memories of old people still alive.

A few weeks later I was speaking to a group of students in one of the most beautiful public libraries I know, formerly the Church of Ireland in Claremorris. It still sits as naturally as a dolmen in a field, even in its metamorphosis, and during a pause, as somebody was searching for a word, a local poet said 'Behind us there where the high altar was, Dónal an Rópa is buried'. There we were, with the April rain falling thickly outside and a friendly glow of light within, and there he was, the Hanging Judge (or rather the bones of him) behind us. The poet's remembrance of Dónal an Rópa was a sort of pardon.

In Kiltimagh there were stories of the blind poet Raftery, who died in 1835. He was born outside that little town and, indeed, more or less banished from it by his patron Frank Taaffe for stealing and selling the man's favourite horse during a bout of drinking. The woods which gave Kiltimagh its name and the blossomy fields of May were to haunt Raftery's verses for the rest of his life, although he probably never went home again. He's at home now around the walls of Walsh's pub in Kiltimagh and there's a fine memorial stone to him in the little town. I learned a great deal of Mayo lore from Ernie Sweeney, a Castlebar man who was illiterate until he was well into his twenties, and who is now a writer remarkable both for his knowledge and critical appreciation of other writers and for his intimate acquaintance with his own county of Mayo. Walking with Ernie on a mountain top or along the bed of a river is a geological and historic feast which nobody who has shared it is likely to forget, but you can't even walk the streets of his own town with the man and not see them with a century or two peeled away as he talks. I can compare him only in this respect with two much-loved friends of one another and of mine, the late Ben Kiely and the late Sean J White.

One morning Ernie Sweeney walked into my office in the Town Hall and said, 'Have you five minutes to spare?' In that five-to seven-minute walk I learned how Lord Lucan turned the course of the Castlebar river away from what is now the main street because he wanted to make use of the land and I saw the only house in Ireland with a river running under it. It's a shop now in Bridge Street with a prettily scrolled frontage surrounding the date 1925, the year I was born.

I learned that the barracks high behind the main street was built from materials torn from Barry's Castle (Caisleán an Bhairaigh) which gave Castlebar its name, and I saw some of the remaining red sandstone paving slabs, and the classical pediment of the Protestant church (all that remains of it) rising behind the house where the rector lived, and the little row of soldiers' houses, soon to be demolished. 'It's like a tidy little English village, or it was' said Ernie, shrewdly indicating the modest Big House set back in its ruined lawns behind a *For Sale* notice on the gatepost. Ernie Sweeney knows his own town, blood and bones, and he loves every inch of it.

One warm April night in the Imperial Hotel, Castlebar-born John Chambers gave a poetry reading which suddenly and terrifyingly illuminated a bald sentence in the booklet that Ernie Sweeney had written for the Adult Literacy Agency to explain how his failure to achieve literacy came about. The sentence is: 'Then I had an accident when I was nine.' John Chambers's poem 'The Ash Pit' had a profound effect on his audience that night. Its setting was the Courthouse just across the Mall from where we sat:

Each night Johnnie cleared the grates,
Forty Courthouse fires,
His bucket like a comet spitting sparks;
His wake across the darkened council yard.
Each night I tagged along
Homework graced until the job was done,
Across tarmac to the pit
Which rumbled
Subterranean, a mass of menace.
With each upturned load
A spill of embers jewelled in the night
Wriggled like insects through ash
Left no trace...
Ernie Sweeney, one evening in the Fall
Boxing Carolan's orchard
Used the wall to cross the garden gate.
He was above me in school,
At jobs like this that tested every rule.
My father saw him fall
Burst the yellow greyish skin,

194

Pluming dust and sparks and screams.
I saw the burns through sleeves and pants.
They had to cut his rubber boots

(Johnny used our kitchen knife)
To free trapped coals;
Red as the screams his mouth kept shaping
His head rocking with the pain.

There was total silence in that upper room as John Chambers read his closing lines. You could feel the moment when art and life came frighteningly together.

The grown man who had been the nine-year-old boxer of orchards was sitting right in front of the poet, head thrown back, listening. He hadn't known that the story of how he came to lose his place in class had ever been told in accomplished verse, or in any other way. This was a dramatic and curiously moving moment in the domestic history of Castlebar. I was very glad to be there.

I was glad throughout my three spells of residence to be in all sorts of other places too. To finish the story of Ernie Sweeney: I was glad one rainy morning to be shown, just outside the town, a grave 'nearly as good as new, with a fine limestone memorial only used on the one side', as Ernie said. He was negotiating with a lady to buy her husband's grave which had been occupied for a short time only, before she decided to move him someplace else. With a showman's flourish, Ernie Sweeney lay down on the grave stone to show me how well it fitted him, and then indicated with his blackthorn stick the first thing he would see at the blowing of the Last Trumpet. It was Nephin Mountain, a fine thing, as he said, to be the first sight a person would see.

Then another day, there was the sight of Belmullet in breezy sun and flying clouds when the little local library building was a very basic structure indeed but full of enthusiastic learners. One October night there was the tiny storm-swept Gaeltacht of Ross Port where the merest handful of aspiring writers, young and old, braved the dark miles on their bicycles to be with us.

At last, a couple of weeks later, I was glad to be up among the hills of Crossmolina and in Ballyhaunis and to be out at last with the mobile library crew on a visit I'll never forget at Achill. As we pulled in to Achill Sound, we heard the uproariously delighted shouts of children just out from school, who came swarming aboard to change their books. Nor will I forget the warmth and hospitality of another visit under the auspices of Joe Daly and Scoil Acla when my friend Marion Fitzgibbon came down from the Arts Council and the celebrations went on into the small hours of the morning.

So concentrated and absorbing was so much of my work as Writer-in-Residence that it wasn't too difficult to put behind me the family tragedy that eventually I would have to face in Dublin. It was obvious to us all that Maurice was growing ever frailer.

After Christmas, in the bleak opening days of 1988, I decided to postpone the next semester in Mayo until Maurice got stronger after a bout of bronchitis aggravated by the chronic emphysema that was slowly bringing him down. He seemed, however, to be much better towards the end of January and (urged by himself) I went back. But that particular period of residence lasted only one night. There was a phone call the next morning whose seriousness I could judge simply by the fact that it was made. Once more I took the rocky road for Dublin, and found that Maurice had been saved from death the previous day when Conor had made a 999 call for the ambulance which rushed him to hospital. I found him there. Suddenly the agreeable and even absorbing life I had planned to pursue in Mayo seemed to me incredibly selfish and frivolous. Also unreal. Reality was here beside me fighting for every breath, with the aid of an oxygen mask. Maurice was being fed through a drip, but, worst of all, he was sometimes attempting to push away the oxygen. I thought I could understand what must be going on inside his wilful head. If this is what attaches me to life, then let me out of this tiresome business of living – if that's what you call it. I couldn't even count on being heard when I tried to talk to him, because his deafness was growing worse with every passing day. He had always detested using a hearing aid, saying it distorted everything.

If he was not an ideal patient, why should he be? Was he not the man who had defined an optimist as somebody who hasn't yet heard the bad news? I felt helpless as I put words into his silence, and watched the firmly closed eyelids with a kind of despair.

On the phone that night, after a discussion with Maurice's doctor, I told Pat McMahon that there was no hope of my going back until after St Patrick's Day, and I offered him two six-week periods of residence to coincide with the school terms, one beginning on 19 March and the other on 1 September. The wonderfully understanding man agreed, although doubtless he would have to justify this to the Council.

At home we all set about plans to drag Maurice back to health once again, and indeed the signs in a day or two were quite hopeful. He hadn't smoked since 19 February, and soon he would be home again. It was, of course, too much to hope that the cursed fags would ever let him free, and, in any event, their damage was so deeply wrought that stopping might not have had much effect. He was never to regain the relative vigour he had enjoyed before that first major collapse in 1988. But he did struggle back to a certain measure of mobility and almost all his mental acuity. By 1989 I had enough confidence in his strength to pay a repeat visit to Zurich and on from there to Venice.

In 1983 I had made the first of quite a few visits to Zurich at the invitation of my friends Ruth Frehner and the late lamented Max Kull. I was booked at the Joyce Foundation to speak about the influence of Joyce on my own first steps as a writer, and I was eager to retrace *his* steps when he first arrived there with Nora Barnacle in 1904. How was it that Zurich could preserve its own past with determination and elegance, and even incorporate into its fabric a bit of Dublin's past, that old oak-panelled bar from Jurys Hotel in Dame Street? With help Professor Fritz Senn had got from a Swiss bank, that powerful piece of nostalgia was transported bit by bit to Zurich, to keep the ghost of Joyce company perhaps. In that beautiful city, which had provided a living of sorts for him when he came with Nora as a very new graduate, Joyce died in 1941, and is buried on a hillside overlooking the lake in Fluntern Cemetery. It was moving to see the famous little bronze at last which marks his grave.

Ruth and I gave him two stolen red roses into his hand, which he didn't reject. We fancied he might even think more of them because they had come from a garden that wasn't ours. The bronze statue by Hebeld is a little smaller than lifesize: Joyce sitting with one ankle resting on his right knee, brooding myopically up there above the Zoo. 'Jim will love to hear the lions roaring', Nora is reported to have said, but personally I doubt if he would. He was even terrified of dogs.

I found it fascinating to reflect that the celebration of this unpredictable foreigner started to be made in Zurich when Joyce was widely unknown and by some people, reviled in his native city. It was, however, a Dublin writer called John Ryan who gave 16 June its label of 'Bloomsday' and who orchestrated the very first celebration of it. He hired a horsedrawn cab and led his friends from one of Bloom's numerous stops to another, many of them pubs, which had, of course, to be revisited. One of them was by this time, John's own pub and restaurant, 'The Bailey'.

But, even at this remove, Zurich is still the real centre for Joycean studies, and the library at the Joyce Foundation, just off Bahnhoffstrasse, contains thousands of volumes of Joyceana.

During the summer of 1989 I was again a guest speaker at the Foundation one breathlessly hot night which ended with an invitation to join a small group of the faithful at the home of Guido Worth. He lived some five or six kilometres outside the city, and he gathered a dozen or so of us onto a traffic island on Bahnhoffstrasse and bought an equivalent number of tickets at the dispensing machine. These he handed one to each of us, and we stood about, confidently awaiting proof of the acknowledged reliability of Swiss transport. But you must understand that this was late at night by Swiss standards, although the beautiful street was still buzzing anng to do with the crowd's reluctance to go home. But Guido was worried. He offered a couple of times to bring us home by taxi and there *were* quite a few taxis awaiting fares. We refused the extravagance in unison and at last the number 8 tram arrived.

Guido gathered his guests around him at the end of the line and we tramped along after him for one of the most unusual parties I have ever attended. The house was in darkness, and when Guido put his key in the door it was obvious that he had recently moved in – suitcases and boxes were everywhere. But he led the way into a huge double room where there was a grand piano and many more unpacked boxes. Chairs were carried in from another room and our host opened up one of the boxes which contained a marvellous selection of exotic dried fruits and nuts (especially imported, somebody told me). Plates were unpacked and handed around, and then glasses were found for a case of Joyce's favourite white wine (Fondant de Sion) which was opened and poured in due course. By this time Guido had sat down at the piano and struck up 'Love's Old Sweet Song' which everybody seemed to know and I got the weird impression that Gabriel Conroy's aunts were somewhere just out of sight and might well join in the chorus. The charm of this evening, which went on into the small hours, was its informality, and the fact that Joyce was being honoured on Bloomsday, in the city that was home to him in the beginning and at the end of his life.

I suppose that it's because my thoughts flew back to 'The

Dead' that I thought also of Maurice – who, to be fair, would have hated an evening like this – and to the bleak realisation that for him holidays and work trips alike were over, and life had narrowed to a circle of light from a reading lamp, to a small grey cloud of smoke from his cigarette and to the purring of his two cats. I might as usual try to recreate this and other holidays for him with what verbal skill I could muster, and I might bring home dozens of photographs for a series of albums in which he delighted, but there was nothing more I or any of us could do for him, except be at home for most of his remaining lease of life. How long or short that would be, we could only conjecture.

In Memoriam

I had thought human ashes would be soft and feathery – that, if one lifted up a handful and let it fall, it would touch down silently, even as the dead themselves. So it took me by surprise when a handful of Maurice's ashes rattled as it was gathered up, rattled thinly as it fell, and then I remembered what I should have known. Just as I had learned everything else of a practical nature from him, I had learned that too.

'Of course human ashes are not soft and feathery, like wood-ash or turf', he had laughed. 'You have to remember that they're composed not just of soft flesh, but of tough bones. Bones that have been pulverised in a furnace, whose fragments (which look a bit like very coarse grey salt) are still hard.'

And his were. They rattled as I lifted them, like the small white pebbles on the beach opposite his grandparents' house in Youghal. I let one handful of them fall at the bottom of the long garden where once he had grown raspberries which, after a shower of July rain, had steamed and ripened under the sun. Now three of his beloved cats were planted there. He had buried the cats himself (Lolita, Umbrage and Keating) each wrapped in the small blanket or jersey it had chosen to steal for its bed. So the little bones of the cats, not pulverised like his own, but probably clean and intact by now, would receive what remained of him when the rains (of how many winters?) had washed them down.

Another handful I scattered under the Beech tree at the front of the house, a mighty tree that predated number thirteen by some twenty years. One mild February day after I'd driven

Maurice home from hospital, I looked at him standing small under that tree (he used to be a tall man) and gazing up into it. He had refused to come with me into the house straight away.

'I need a mouthful of fresh air,' he'd said, 'after that overheated bloody place.'

But he didn't allow himself very much fresh air. When I looked out from an upper window, the smoke from his forbidden cigarette was rising up and vanishing into the lower branches of the tree which was at last quickening into some signs of spring. The Beech is a late bloomer, seldom wakening up before the end of April. He would last long enough to look up, as we all did every year, into the cathedral of young leaves. So I thought, and I wasn't wrong. But he didn't last long enough to see the autumn glory swept away. Some of it still lay in rusty golden drifts under the November sky the day he set off for the last time in his newest old car. He didn't call back to me in the garden as he usually did, to know if there was anything we needed from the shops. That was because he wasn't, as it happened, going to the shops that day. It was from the nearby Dublin mountains, from the car park on the steep track up to the Hellfire Club in fact, that he had been carried down by ambulance to the hospital, and he lived for two more weeks.

'I botched it, love', he said to me, in the Casualty Ward. 'Forgive me for bringing all this bloody mess on all of you.' Speechless we held him, his sons and I. His forehead was cut and bleeding because, as he lost consciousness, he had fallen against the door of the car. The cut was deep and needed a few stitches. It had all healed up beautifully in time for him to die. The human body is a strange and contrary thing. He would have been the first to point out to us the necessity as well as the futility of all that frenzy of healing. And, inevitably, a medical student's pal as well as a student of science, he would have given us the explanation. Instead, all that sophisticated intelligence, all that black humour and kindness, and all that wisdom went into a bath of formaldehyde in the Royal College of Surgeons to be studied by merrily quipping students like his long-ago friend. This donation of his body was according to his Will, made some twenty years previously when he was not yet fifty.

It was eighteen months before they gave us back what remained of him for cremation. When he died he was sixty-seven years old, and he and I had spent thirty-nine of those years together in the house behind the Beech tree. There he had written, a few months before we were married, an internationally acknowledged masterpiece called *Vladivostok*, but he had taken too literally a sentence from Cyril Connolly's *The Unquiet Grave*, and he had written hardly anything else afterwards. I haven't forgotten that sentence, because he was always quoting it: 'The more books we read, the sooner we perceive that the only function of a writer is to produce a masterpiece. No other task is of any consequence.'

In a way, not just *Vladivostok* but Maurice Kennedy's life, and even his carefully contrived death, were masterpieces of understatement.

– fin –

451
Editions